D1827676

'I HAVE WRITTEN TO THE KING, MY LORD'

Hebrew Bible Monographs, 1

Series Editors
David J.A. Clines
J. Cheryl Exum
Keith W. Whitelam

'I HAVE WRITTEN TO THE KING, MY LORD'

Secular Analogies for the Psalms

Roger Tomes

SHEFFIELD PHOENIX PRESS

2005

Copyright © 2005, 2006 Sheffield Phoenix Press

First published in hardback, 2005
First published in paperback, 2006

Published by Sheffield Phoenix Press
Department of Biblical Studies, University of Sheffield
Sheffield S10 2TN

www.sheffieldphoenix.com

All rights reserved.
No part of this publication may be reproduced or transmitted in any form or by any
means, electronic or mechanical, including photocopying, recording or any information
storage or retrieval system, without the publishers' permission in writing.

A CIP catalogue record for this book
is available from the British Library

Typeset by Forthcoming Publications
Printed by Lightning Source

ISBN 1-905048-092 (hardback)
ISBN 1-905048-71-8 (paperback)
ISSN 1747-9614

CONTENTS

ABBREVIATIONS

ABL	R.F. Harper, *Assyrian and Babylonian Letters* (14 vols.; London: British Museum; Chicago: University of Chicago Press, 1892–1914)
AEM	*Archives Épistolaires de Mari* (Archives royales de Mari, XXVI; Paris: Editions Recherche sur les Civilisations, 1988)
AfO	*Archiv für Orientforschung*
AJSL	*American Journal of Semitic Languages and Literatures*
AnBib	Analecta biblica
ANET	James B. Pritchard (ed.), *Ancient Near Eastern Texts Relating to the Old Testament* (Princeton, NJ: Princeton University Press, 1950)
AOAT	Alter Orient und Altes Testament
AOTS	D. Winton Thomas, *Archaeology and Old Testament Study* (Oxford: Clarendon Press, 1967)
ARAB	D.D. Luckenbill, *Ancient Records of Assyria and Babylonia* (2 vols.; Chicago: University of Chicago Press, 1926–27)
ARE	J.H. Breasted, *Ancient Records of Egypt* (5 vols.; Chicago: University of Chicago Press, 1906–1907)
ARM	Archives royales de Mari
ARW	*Archiv für Religionswissenschaft*
BA	*Biblical Archaeologist*
BASOR	*Bulletin of the American Schools of Oriental Research*
Before the Muses	B.R. Foster, *Before the Muses: An Anthology of Akkadian Literature* (2 vols.; Bethesda, MD: CDL Press, 2nd edn, 1996)
BM	Egyptian Holdings in the British Museum
BZAW	*Beihefte zur ZAW*
CAD	Ignace I. Gelb *et al.* (eds.), *The Assyrian Dictionary of the Oriental Institute of the University of Chicago* (Chicago: Oriental Institute, 1964–)
CAH	Cambridge Ancient History
CH	Code of Hammurabi
CoS	W.W. Hallo and K.R. Younger (eds.), *The Context of Scripture*. I. *Canonical Compositions from the Biblical World* (Leiden: E.J. Brill, 1996); II. *Monumental Inscriptions from the Biblical World* (1997); III. *Archival Documents from the Biblical World* (2000).
CT	Cuneiform Texts from Babylonian Tablets, etc., in the British Museum, 1896–

CTH	E. Laroche, *Catalogue des textes hittites* (Études et commentaires 75; Paris: Éditions Klincksieck, 1971)
DEPM	J.-M. Durand, *Les documents épistolaires du palais de Mari* (Littératures anciennes du Proche-Orient, 16-18; Paris: Cerf; I, 1997; II, 1998; III, 2000)
DOTT	D. Winton Thomas (ed.), *Documents from Old Testament Times* (London: Thomas Nelson, 1958)
EA	Amarna tablets
ET	English translation
FOTL	The Forms of the Old Testament Literature
FRLANT	Forschungen zur Religion und Literatur des Alten und Neuen Testaments
HAT	Handbuch zum Alten Testament
HDT	Gary Beckman, *Hittite Diplomatic Texts* (SBL Writings from the Ancient World, 7; Atlanta: Scholars Press, 2nd edn, 1999)
HKAT	Handkommentar zum Alten Testament
HPD	M.-J. Seux (ed.), *Hymnes et prières aux dieux de Babylonie et d'Assyrie* (Littératures anciennes du Proche-Orient, 8; Paris: Cerf, 1976)
HTR	*Harvard Theological Review*
HUCA	*Hebrew Union College Annual*
Int	*Interpretation*
JAOS	*Journal of the American Oriental Society*
JBL	*Journal of Biblical Literature*
JCS	*Journal of Cuneiform Studies*
JEA	*Journal of Egyptian Archaeology*
JNES	*Journal of Near Eastern Studies*
JSOT	*Journal for the Study of the Old Testament*
JSOTSup	*Journal for the Study of the Old Testament*, Supplement Series
KBo	Keilschrifttexte aus Boghazköi, I–VI (Wissenschaftliche Veröffenlichungen des deutschen Orient-Gesellschaft 30 [1916]; 36 [1921])
LAS	S. Parpola, *Letters from Assyrian Scholars to the Kings Esarhaddon and Assurbanipal* (AOAT, 5; Neukirchen–Vluyn: Neukirchener Verlag, I [Texts], 1970; II [Commentary and Appendices], 1983)
ND	Cuneiform Texts from Nimrud
OBO	Orbis biblicus et orientalis
OECT	Oxford Editions of Cuneiform Texts
OLZ	*Orientalistische Literaturzeitung*
OTL	Old Testament Library
Prosopography	Karen Radner *et al.* (eds.), *The Prosopography of the Neo-Assyrian Empire* I.1: A; I.2: B-G; II.2: L-N; III.1: P-S (Helsinki: Neo-Assyrian Text Corpus Project, 1998–)
PRU	*Le palais royal d'Ugarit*
RB	*Revue biblique*

RS	Ras Shamra texts
SAA	State Archives of Assyria
SAHG	A. Falkenstein and W. von Soden, *Sumerische und akkadische Hymnen und Gebete* (Die Bibliothek der alten Welt; Zürich: Artemis-Verlag, 1953)
SBL	Society of Biblical Literature
SBLDS	SBL Dissertation Series
SJT	*Scottish Journal of Theology*
TBü	Theologische Bücherei
THAT	Ernst Jenni and Claus Westermann (eds.), *Theologisches Handwörterbuch zum Alten Testament* (2 vols.; Munich: Chr. Kaiser Verlag, 1971–76)
TynBul	*Tyndale Bulletin*
VAB	Vorderasiatische Bibliothek
VT	*Vetus Testamentum*
WMANT	Wissenschaftliche Monographien zum Alten und Neuen Testament
ZAW	*Zeitschrift für die alttestamentliche Wissenschaft*
ZDMG	*Zeitschrift der deutschen morgenländischen Gesellschaft*
ZThK	*Zeitschrift für Theologie und Kirche*

PREFACE

This study is the product of both my youth and my age. It began as a chapter in my Oxford BD thesis of 1963. Professor John Emerton encouraged me to develop it, which I did, using the resources of the University of London Senate House Library, during the next ten years. Then, because of the demands of a pastorate and those of teaching at Northern College and the University of Manchester, it was set aside until my retirement in 1993. Bringing it up to date in the light of more recent work on the Psalms, and with the help of the excellent editions of the ancient Near Eastern material that have become available, has been a rewarding task, though perhaps not carried through as thoroughly as I would have wished. Critics may be able to detect passages that still reflect the outlook and concerns of a generation ago.

I should like to thank Professors John Emerton, Kenneth Kitchen, Wilfred Lambert and Alan Millard for sharing their expertise so generously with me; Professor David Clines for accepting the study for publication; Dr Adrian Curtis and Dr Jack McKelvey for the loan of books; and the Document Supply Unit of the John Rylands University of Manchester for the trouble they have taken to procure the material I needed.

I should also like to thank the Society for Old Testament Study and the Ehrhardt Seminar of the Centre for Biblical Studies in the University of Manchester for the intellectual stimulus they have provided over many years. The Appendix was read as my first paper to the Society in 1974 and the Ehrhardt Seminar commented on a summary version of this study when I was beginning to revise it. The Centre's kindness in making me an Honorary Research Fellow has greatly facilitated my work and is a privilege I value.

Finally, I should like to thank my wife, Yvonne, with whom I have recently celebrated fifty years of marriage, for not begrudging me the time to finish the book.

October 2004

ACKNOWLEDGMENTS

Permission to use copyright material has been granted by the following:

The Oriental Institute of the University of Chicago for quotations from the translations by A. Leo Oppenheim in *Letters from Mesopotamia.*

Helsinki University Press for quotations from the translations in the several volumes in the State Archives of Assyria series.

The British School of Archaeology in Iraq for quotations from the *Nimrud Letters* (CTN 5), edited by H.W.F. Saggs.

The Johns Hopkins University Press for quotations from the translations by W.L. Moran in *The Amarna Letters.*

1

COMPARATIVE STUDY OF THE PSALMS

This study is an attempt to explain certain elements in Old Testament prayers, particularly in the so-called 'individual laments' (or 'complaints') in the Psalter, from comparative ancient Near Eastern material. It is by no means the first of its kind: there have been a number of such studies, some of them detailed and important, in the twentieth century.[1]

Hitherto, as is natural, the chief concern has been the direct comparison of the psalms with the religious texts of Mesopotamia, Egypt and Canaan. From Mesopotamia and Egypt have come considerable numbers of texts comparable to the psalms in literary type, poetic form, content and expression. Thus in 1922 F. Stummer[2] analysed a typical Akkadian *šu-illa*—a prayer to Šamaš for protection against the misfortune presaged by a serpent[3]—and was able to show that most of its structural elements (address to the deity, description of

---

1. For a survey of the work done up to 1951, see A.R. Johnson, 'The Psalms', in H.H. Rowley (ed.), *The Old Testament and Modern Study* (Oxford: Clarendon Press, 1951), pp. 162-209 (186-89).
2. F. Stummer, *Sumerische–akkadische Parallelen zum Aufbau alttestamentlicher Psalmen* (Studien zur Geschichte und Kultur des Altertums, 11; Paderborn: Schöningh, 1922).
3. A. Falkenstein and W. von Soden (eds.), *Sumerische und akkadische Hymnen und Gebete* (Die Bibliothek der alten Welt; Zürich: Artemis-Verlag, 1953) (*SAHG*), B 55; M.-J. Seux (ed.), *Hymnes et prières aux dieux de Babylonie et d'Assyrie* (Littératures anciennes du Proche-Orient, 8; Paris: Cerf, 1976) (= *HPD*), pp. 364-65; B.R. Foster, *Before the Muses: An Anthology of Akkadian Literature* (2 vols.; Bethesda, MD: CDL Press, 2nd edn, 1996), III.50(c), p. 635. The name *šu-illa* means '(prayer with) uplifted hands'. On the *šu-illa* type see Walter G. Kunstmann, *Die babylonische Gebetsbeschwörung* (Leipziger Semitische Studien, NF 2; Leipzig: J.C. Hinrichs, 1932); *SAHG*, pp. 46-47, 295-394 (Nos. B 40-81); E. Ebeling, *Die akkadische Gebetsserie 'Handerhebung'* (Deutsche Akademie der Wissenschaften zu Berlin, Institut für Orientforschung, Veröffentlichung, 20; Berlin: Akademie-Verlag, 1953); E.R. Dalglish, *Psalm Fifty-One in the Light of Ancient Near Eastern Patternism* (Leiden: E.J. Brill, 1962), pp. 41-51; A.L. Oppenheim, *Ancient Mesopotamia: Portrait of a Dead Civilization* (Chicago: University of Chicago Press, 1964), pp. 270-71; *HPD*, pp. 24-27, 269-346.

his majesty, worshipper's introduction of himself, description of distress, petition and concluding promise) and some of its motifs (rhetorical questions, reproachful questions, expression of certainty that the prayer has been heard) were also to be found in Israelite psalms.[4] In 1926 H. Gressmann, G.R. Driver and A.M. Blackman collected together the most striking examples of the way in which Babylonian and Egyptian research shed light on the form and content of the psalms, though without limiting themselves to directly comparable psalm material.[5] In 1928 J. Begrich[6] compared the expressions of trust in the deity in the Akkadian *šu-illa* and the Israelite individual lament. Gunkel's commentary on the Psalms, published in 1926,[7] was the first to make detailed use of comparative material, and in the introduction to that commentary, completed after Gunkel's death by Begrich,[8] the detailed analysis of each psalm type is illustrated at every point from the Babylonian and Egyptian literatures. In 1934 C.G. Cumming[9] compared the poetic form, phraseology and religious ideas of the Akkadian and Hebrew hymns, and in 1936 G. Widengren[10] compared the Akkadian and Hebrew laments, using a scheme of analysis similar to that of Stummer, but with much fuller citation of parallels and with special attention to the religious ideas expressed. Widengren may perhaps be criticised for quoting indiscriminately from various types of Akkadian psalm,[11] though it has not been shown that this has led to any serious misinterpretation of the Akkadian material. Some of his discussions are extended and valuable, for example, those on the reason for the praise of the deity (pp. 40-43), the character of God (pp. 49-52, 316-17),

---

4.   Stummer also analysed an *er-šemma*, 'lament to the flute', as a liturgy for public worship.

5.   H. Gressmann, 'The Development of Hebrew Psalmody'; G.R. Driver, 'The Psalms in the Light of Babylonian Research'; A.M. Blackman, 'The Psalms in the Light of Egyptian Research', in D.C. Simpson (ed.), *The Psalmists* (London: Oxford University Press, 1926), pp. 1-21 (15-20), 109-75, 177-97, respectively.

6.   J. Begrich, 'Die Vertrauensäusserungen im israelitischen Klagelied des Einzelnen und in seinen babylonischen Gegenstücken', *ZAW* 46 (1928), pp. 221-60; reprinted in *Gesammelte Studien zum Alten Testament* (TBü, 21; Munich: Chr. Kaiser Verlag, 1964), pp. 168-216.

7.   H. Gunkel, *Die Psalmen* (HKAT, II/2; Göttingen: Vandenhoeck & Ruprecht, 1926).

8.   H. Gunkel and J. Begrich, *Einleitung in die Psalmen* (Göttingen: Vandenhoeck & Ruprecht, 1933; ET James D. Nogalski, *Introduction to Psalms: The Genres of the Religious Lyrics of Israel* [Mercer Library of Biblical Studies; Macon, GA: Mercer University Press, 1998]). References will be to chapter and section, common to the German and the English translation.

9.   C.G. Cumming, *The Assyrian and Hebrew Hymns of Praise* (Columbia University Oriental Studies, 12; New York: Columbia University Press, 1934).

10.   G. Widengren, *The Akkadian and Hebrew Psalms of Lamentation as Religious Documents: A Comparative Study* (Stockholm: Bokförlags Aktiebolaget Thule, 1937).

11.   Dalglish, *Psalm Fifty-One*, p. 250.

monotheism (pp. 54-55), trust in God (pp. 80-81), the aloofness of God (pp. 137-39), penitence (pp. 140-62), the connection between suffering and sin (pp. 162-96), the identification of the evils complained of (pp. 197-250), and seeing the face of God (pp. 251-57). G.R. Castellino's brief study[12] (1940) is an analysis of typical examples of the Akkadian *šu-illa*[13] and hymn and their Old Testament counterparts. C. Westermann included in his book on the praise of God in the Psalms, first published in 1953, a brief comparison with Babylonian and Egyptian psalms.[14] In the study by E.R. Dalglish Psalm 51 is interpreted in detail in the light of the Babylonian penitential psalms (the Sumerian and Akkadian *šu-illa* and the Sumerian *eršahunga*, 'song to appease the heart'); and in that by A. Barucq,[15] after a review of previous work, the Old Testament hymns and prayers are compared in detail with corresponding Egyptian material.

There were fewer comparative studies of this kind in the second half of the twentieth century. A notable exception was E.S. Gerstenberger's *Der bittende Mensch*,[16] which includes an analysis (pp. 64-112) of the *Sitz im Leben* of the Babylonian exorcism prayers. The prayers are seen to be part of an elaborate ritual, which included sacrifice and various apotropaic acts, diagnosis and therapy. They are the work of the specialists who devised and supervised the ritual. However, they are not part of the official temple cult: the ritual is carried out within the primary group in which the sufferer lives. Gerstenberger argues (pp. 113-60) that the individual laments in the Psalter were similarly devised by priests or prophets for local use.

More recently there has been interest in comparing the structure, themes and occasions of the communal laments of Mesopotamia—the Sumerian city-laments and *balag* and *eršemma* laments—with those of the communal laments in the Psalter and Lamentations. This has been prompted by the publication of new editions of the Sumerian material first published early in the twentieth century[17] and by the publication of texts hitherto unavailable.[18]

---

12. G.R. Castellino, *Le lamentazioni individuali e gli Inni in Babilonia e in Israele* (Turin: Societa Editrice Internationale, 1940).

13. J. Böllenrücher, *Gebete und Hymnen an Nergal* (Leipzig: J.C. Hinrichs, 1904), No.1.

14. C. Westermann, *Das Loben Gottes in den Psalmen* (Göttingen: Vandenhoeck & Ruprecht, 2nd edn, 1961; ET *The Praise of God in the Psalms* [London: Epworth Press, 1966]), pp. 36-51; reprinted in *idem, Praise and Lament in the Psalms* (Edinburgh: T. & T. Clark, 1981), pp. 36-51.

15. A. Barucq, *L'expression de la louange divine et de la prière dans la Bible et en Égypte* (Bibliothèque d'étude, 33; Cairo: Institut français d'archéologie orientale, 1962).

16. E.S. Gerstenberger, *Der bittende Mensch: Bittritual und Klagelied des Einzelnen im Alten Testament* (WMANT, 51; Neukirchen–Vluyn: Neukirchener Verlag, 1980).

17. For example by S. Langdon, *Sumerian and Babylonian Psalms* (Paris: Librairie Paul Geuthner, 1909); *idem, Babylonian Liturgies* (Paris: Librairie Paul Geuthner, 1913).

Despite the distance in time and space between the Sumerian laments and the Hebrew laments[19]—the Sumerian laments derive from the Old Babylonian period (2000–1600 BCE)[20]—and differences in style and theology—the prevalence of catalogues and the intercession of one god with another in the Sumerian laments[21]—there are obvious points of comparison. The biblical Lamentations is a series of laments for the fall of a city;[22] all the laments characteristically contain the elements of praise, descriptive narrative and entreaty.[23]

It is clear from the work that has been done that the parallels between the Old Testament psalms and their Mesopotamian and Egyptian counterparts are rarely close enough for us to suppose that the Hebrew psalms are translations or adaptations of foreign texts. The only instance in which direct literary dependence is at all probable is that of Psalm 104 and the Hymn to Aten.[24] Otherwise it would be difficult to maintain that any Hebrew psalmist had direct knowledge of any particular Mesopotamian or Egyptian text. Indeed, several of the scholars mentioned above have pointed out that the differences between the biblical psalms and their ancient Near Eastern counterparts are as striking as the resemblances. Begrich, for example, found the expressions of trust in the Psalms more colourful, less stereotyped than in the Akkadian *šu-illa*; whereas in the latter trust was only a subordinate motif, in the Psalms it was dominant.[25] Castellino, contrasting the *šu-illa* and the individual lament

18. S.N. Kramer, *Lamentation over the Destruction of Ur* (Assyriological Studies, 12; Chicago: Chicago University Press, 1940; translation by Kramer in *ANET*, pp. 455-63); 'Lamentation over the Destruction of Sumer and Ur', in *ANET*, pp. 611-19; J. Krecher, *Sumerische Kultlyrik* (Wiesbaden: Otto Harrassowitz, 1966); R. Kutscher, *Oh Angry Sea: The History of a Sumerian Congregational Lament* (Yale Near Eastern Researches, 6; New Haven: Yale University Press, 1975); M.E. Cohen, *Sumerian Hymnology: The eršemma* (HUCA Supplement, 2; Cincinnati: Hebrew Union College, 1981); *idem, The Canonical Lamentations of Ancient Mesopotamia* (2 vols.; Potomac, MD; Capital Decisions, 1988); M. Green, 'The Eridu Lament', *JCS* 30 (1978), pp. 127-67; *idem*, 'The Uruk Lament', *JAOS* 104 (1984), pp. 252-79.

19. T.F. McDaniel, 'The Alleged Sumerian Influence upon Lamentations', *VT* 18 (1968), pp. 198-209 (207-208).

20. Cohen, *Canonical Lamentations*, p. 11.

21. P.W. Ferris, Jr, *The Genre of Communal Lament in the Bible and the Ancient Near East* (Atlanta: Scholars Press, 1992), p. 173, lists a number of features of the Sumerian communal laments which are 'noticeably absent' from the Hebrew laments.

22. W.C. Gwaltney, Jr, 'The Biblical Book of Lamentations in the Context of Near Eastern Lament Literature', in W.W. Hallo, J.C. Moyer and L.G. Perdue (eds.), *Scripture in Context. II. More Essays on the Comparative Method* (Winona Lake, IN: Eisenbrauns, 1983), pp. 191-211.

23. Ferris, *Genre*, p. 162.

24. See, e.g., R.J. Williams, 'The Hymn to Aten', in *DOTT*, pp. 142-50.

25. Begrich, 'DieVertrauensäusserungen', pp. 259-60.

more generally, noted that in the Babylonian prayer there was mention of all kinds of evils, natural and supernatural, from gods and demons, enemies, illness, curses, etc., while in the biblical prayer enemies predominated and no supernatural beings other than Yahweh were mentioned; that the Babylonian prayer described symptoms, while the biblical prayer was rarely specific; that the highly metaphorical language of the Psalter was absent from the *šu-illa*; that the Israelite psalms had a flexibility of structure and a variety of expression that the Babylonian psalms lacked; and that magic was prominent in the Babylonian texts but absent from the biblical.[26] Widengren noted that the invocation of the deity was briefer in the biblical psalms.[27] These differences have been noted by Assyriologists as well: B. Landsberger, in a review of Stummer's book, contrasted the free flow of thought of the Psalms with the strict architectonic structure, the closely followed rules of style and the conventional themes of Babylonian hymns and prayers;[28] A. Falkenstein and W. von Soden, in the introduction to their selection of Sumerian and Akkadian hymns and prayers, drew attention to the polytheism of the Akkadian prayers and their attachment to tradition rather than commitment to one God, and to their lack of national consciousness compared with the Israelite psalms.[29] Barucq had similar observations to make on the differences between biblical and Egyptian prayers: in Egyptian prayers the requests chiefly concern the life beyond; direct imperatives to the deity are avoided; virtuous conduct is stressed rather than innocence of transgression; Israelite prayers are much more personal.[30] Thus any theory of literary dependence would have to reckon, not only with the very general nature of the resemblances, but also with the pronounced differences.

Explanations of Parallels

Nevertheless the parallels, general though they are, are numerous enough and close enough to call for some kind of explanation. They cannot be due merely to coincidence. Poetry does not always mean an arrangement of words in half lines that balance one another in meaning, as it does in both Mesopotamia and Israel. It is not inevitable that a religious literature should possess a category 'psalm' that can be subdivided, however roughly, into hymns, laments and thanksgivings. Not all traditions of prayer give a regular place to protestations of innocence or loyalty or to the reproachful questions 'Why?' and

26. Castellino, *Lamentazioni*, p. 16.
27. Widengren, *Psalms of Lamentation*, p. 40; cf. Dalglish, *Psalm Fifty-One*, pp. 259-60.
28. *OLZ* 28 (1925), cols. 479-83 (479).
29. *SAHG*, pp. 55-56.
30. Barucq, *L'expression*, pp. 24, 28, 502-505.

'How long?'. Resemblances of this character may not suggest direct borrowing or adaptation of psalms, but they do suggest a common literary tradition.

The explanations usually advanced for these resemblances are of three kinds: direct literary influence; a common proto-Semitic inheritance; indirect literary influence mediated through Canaan.

The advocates of direct literary influence have pointed out that there were three periods in Israelite history when psalmists could have had direct knowledge of Babylonian or Egyptian psalm writing. During the exile there were Jews in both Babylonia and Egypt, but this period is not favoured because internal evidence suggests that most psalms are pre-exilic.[31]

Judah was open to Assyrian influence from the time of Ahaz onwards;[32] Egyptian influence was probably known from the time of the united monarchy under David and Solomon.[33] There were periods when Akkadian and Egyptian prayers could have been known to Israelite psalmists at first hand and could have provided them with their basic models. The difficulty with this view will always be why the Israelite psalms are not more like their supposed prototypes than they are.

The second explanation is that the resemblances are due to a common proto-Semitic inheritance. Just as the Akkadian and Hebrew languages derive from a common stock, so do their verse forms and parallelism, the impulse to express religious feelings in psalms, the general conception of God's relationship to the world and the serious attitude to sin.[34] Ferris, while conceding that there are 'some very close similarities in style and substance' between the Mesopotamian and biblical communal lament traditions, argues that 'the parallels are best explained as coincidental and the result of a common experience addressed by a similar, if not common, culture'.[35] While the most general points of resemblance may be satisfactorily explained in this way, however, it hardly covers the many echoes in detail, such as the use of the same metaphors.[36] Furthermore, the individual lament as we have it in the Psalter developed relatively late in Israel, certainly after the settlement in Canaan: early Hebrew laments are far less elaborate.[37] Even if Israel's ances-

31. C.J. Gadd, 'The Second Lamentation for Ur', in D.W. Thomas and W.D. McHardy (eds.), *Hebrew and Semitic Studies Presented to Godfrey Rolles Driver* (Oxford: Oxford University Press, 1963), pp. 59-71 (61), suggested that the Babylonian exile provided the opportunity for the Mesopotamian laments to influence the composition of Lamentations.

32. 2 Kgs 16; cf. Stummer, *Parallelen*, p. 4.

33. 1 Kgs 3.1; 7.8; 9.16; 10.28-29; 11.40.

34. G.R. Driver, 'Babylonian Research', p. 173; *SAHG*, p. 55; Dalglish, *Psalm Fifty-One*, p. 254.

35. Ferris, *Genre*, p. 173.

36. *SAHG*, p. 55.

37. Dalglish, *Psalm Fifty-One*, p. 256; cf. A. Wendel, *Das freie Laiengebet in vorexilischen Israel* (Leipzig: E. Pfeiffer, 1931), pp. 123-69; C. Westermann, 'Struktur

tors, or some of them, had a Mesopotamian origin, they did not bring the psalm types fully grown as part of their inheritance.

Hence the third explanation, that the influence of Babylonia and perhaps Egypt as well has been mediated through Canaan, became the most popular.[38] It rests partly on the evidence of the Ras Shamra texts and partly on that of the Amarna letters. The Ras Shamra texts show that there was a Canaanite religious literature, prior to that of Israel in time and much nearer to it in place than the Babylonian and Egyptian literatures. The mythical texts show numerous parallels with the Psalter in vocabulary, style and mythological content.[39] Nevertheless, only three fragments of what seem to be Canaanite psalms are known,[40] and these are insufficient for any significant comparison of Israelite and Canaanite psalmody. It has been argued that certain psalms, for example, Psalm 29, are in origin Canaanite psalms which have been adapted to Israelite use,[41] but this remains a matter of inference. The Ras Shamra evidence fails to provide a prototype for the Israelite individual lament as a whole or to illustrate its characteristic motifs.

The Amarna letters contain passages whose language and metrical structure are reminiscent of passages in the Hebrew psalms. It has been suggested that these are extracts from hymns to a Canaanite god, and only secondarily applied to the pharaoh to whom the letters are written.[42] This theory of quotation from a fixed source would alone suffice to explain how identical passages can appear in different letters from the same writer and even from different writers. That the source is Canaanite is supported by the inclusion of Canaanite glosses for certain words, and by the ease with which the passages in question can be translated into metrical Hebrew. It has been pointed out, however, that the Canaanite glosses and the possibility of translation into

und Geschichte der Klage im Alten Testament', *ZAW* 66 (1954), pp. 44-80 (46-49, 66-69); reprinted in *idem, Forschung am Alten Testament. Gesammelte Studien 1* (TBü, 24; Munich: Chr. Kaiser Verlag, 1954), pp. 266-305 (268-71, 291-94); ET *Praise and Lament in the Psalms*, pp. 165-258 (168-72, 195-99).

38. Driver, 'Babylonian Research', p. 174; Widengren, *Psalms of Lamentation*, pp. 5-16; Dalglish, *Psalm Fifty-One*, pp. 251-52; S. Mowinckel, 'Psalm Criticism between 1900 and 1935 (Ugarit and Psalm Exegesis)', *VT* 5 (1955), pp. 12-33 (22); *idem, The Psalms in Israel's Worship* (trans. D.R. Ap-Thomas; 2 vols.; Oxford: Basil Blackwell, 1962), II, p. 177.

39. See J.H. Patton, *Canaanite Parallels in the Book of Psalms* (Baltimore: The Johns Hopkins University Press, 1944); J. Coppens, 'Les parallèles du psautier avec les textes de Ras Shamra-Ougarit', *Mélanges L.Th. Lefort = Le Muséon* 59 (1946), pp. 113-42.

40. RS 94, 95 (Akkadian); RS 13 + 43 (Ugaritic); see Mowinckel, 'Psalm Criticism', pp. 14-15.

41. H.L. Ginsberg, 'Ugaritic Studies and the Bible' *BA* 8 (1945), pp. 41-58; reprinted in D.N. Freedman and E.F. Campbell (eds.), *The Biblical Archaeologist Reader 2* (Garden City, NY: Doubleday, 1964), pp. 34-50 (45-46).

42. For a fuller treatment of this question, and references, see Appendix.

Hebrew do not *prove* a Canaanite origin, and that there is nothing specifically Canaanite about the content of the passages. No parallels with the Ras Shamra texts have been drawn, and certain phrases are commonly found in Egyptian literature. An alternative suggestion is that there existed 'collections of approved formulas in Akkadian (with or without Canaanite glosses) for official correspondence with the suzerain'.

Secular Analogies

If it is not regarded as established that the 'hymnic' passages in the Amarna letters are secondary applications of hymns to the gods, then we may rather be confronted by an important *secular* analogy to the psalms. Praise of and prayer to the deity are close enough to praise of and appeals to the king for them to sound very much alike.[43] Either psalms are religious versions of secular discourse, or address to the king is modelled on religious discourse. We shall see reason to believe that the priority lies with the secular situation, but at the moment it is sufficient to note that much the same language and many of the same motifs are used in both. It is the purpose of this study to show how this analogy was worked out in detail.

Encouragement to study a secular analogy to a feature of biblical religious life comes from the well known comparison first made by G.E. Mendenhall[44] between the biblical covenant Yahweh made with Israel and the treaties made by Hittite kings with their neighbours and vassals. It is not to be supposed that there has been discovered in the Hittite treaties or in those from Ugarit or Assyria either direct literary sources for any formulation of the biblical covenant or evidence of a strict pattern to which the biblical covenant was bound to conform.[45] Nor does the analogy with Hittite treaties of the second millen-

---

43. Barucq compares hymns to the king in Egypt and hymns to Yahweh in Israel, *L'expression*, pp. 307-11.

44. G.E. Mendenhall, 'Covenant Forms in Israelite Tradition', *BA* 17 (1954), pp. 50-76, reprinted in E.F. Campbell and D.N. Freedman (eds.), *The Biblical Archaeologist Reader 3* (Garden City, NY: Doubleday, 1970), pp. 25-53. According to D.J. McCarthy, *Treaty and Covenant: A Study in Form in the Ancient Oriental Documents and in the Old Testament* (AnBib, 21A; Rome: Biblical Institute Press), p. 3, the coincidence in form between treaty and covenant was first pointed out by E. Bickerman, 'Couper une alliance', *Archive d'histoire du droit oriental* 5 (1951), pp. 133-56 (153-54). In an additional note to a reprint of this article, in *Studies in Jewish and Christian History: Part One* (Arbeiten zur Geschichte des aniken Judentums und des Urchristentums, 9; Leiden: E.J. Brill, 1976), pp. 1-32 (26-32), Bickerman expressed some reservations about the parallels others had drawn between the biblical covenant and the treaties.

45. McCarthy, *Treaty and Covenant*, pp. 5-8, 159; E. Gerstenberger, *Wesen und Herkunft der 'apodiktischen Rechts'* (WMANT, 20; Neukirchen–Vluyn: Neukirchener Verlag, 1965), pp. 96-110; *idem*, 'Covenant and Commandment', *JBL* 84 (1965),

nium prove that the biblical texts, such as the Decalogue and Deuteronomy, are of early date.[46] Nevertheless the discovery of the analogy has in itself made the character of the biblical covenant much more intelligible. Covenant terminology and ideas can now be detected where the word 'covenant' is not expressly used.[47] Many of the great words in Israel's religious vocabulary have their home in the context of the covenant.[48] The comparison of covenant with treaty has thus demonstrated that sometimes the most fruitful analogy for a religious institution is secular rather than religious. Archaeology has hitherto failed to show any example of a *religious* covenant (i.e. between a nation and its god) outside Israel, but even if it had done so, the secular analogy would still be important in its own right, as adding a new dimension to our understanding of religious institutions: relationship to God is conceived and expressed in terms derived from human social relationships. This had of course been pointed out many times before Mendenhall published his article,[49] but only in a very general way: the significance of Mendenhall's contribution and all that has followed from it is that it has demonstrated *in detail*, in one area at least, the truth of the general statement. Its success invites the attempt to explore a detailed secular analogy to another field of biblical religion, such as prayer.

pp. 38-51; H. Reventlow, 'Kultische Recht im Alten Testament', *ZThK* 60 (1963), pp. 267-304 (274-81); R. Smend, *Die Bundesformel* (Theologische Studien, 68; Zürich: EVZ Verlag, 1963), p. 34 n. 16; J. Barr, 'Covenant', in J. Hastings (ed.), *Dictionary of the Bible* (rev. F.C. Grant and H.H. Rowley; Edinburgh: T. & T. Clark, 1963), pp. 183-86 (184a); J.J. Stamm and M.E. Andrew, *The Ten Commandments in Recent Research* (Studies in Biblical Theology, Second Series, 2; London: SCM Press, 1967), p. 68.

46. G. Fohrer, Review of McCarthy, *Treaty and Covenant*, *ZAW* 76 (1964), p. 236.

47. J. Muilenburg, 'The Form and Structure of the Covenantal Formulations', *VT* 9 (1959), pp. 347-65.

48. J.A. Thompson, *The Ancient Near Eastern Treaties and the Old Testament* (London: Tyndale Press, 1964), pp. 35-38; A.R. Millard, 'For He is Good', *TynBul* 17 (1966), pp. 115-17.

49. E.g. by G.E. Wright, 'The Terminology of Old Testament Religion and its Significance', *JNES* 1 (1942), pp. 404-14.

2

OLD TESTAMENT PRAYERS
AND ANCIENT NEAR EASTERN LETTERS

An important passage for understanding the nature of prayer in the Old Testament is the prayer of Solomon at the dedication of the temple (1 Kgs 8.22-53). It is useful because it catalogues the various situations in which prayer would commonly be made. Hans Schmidt[1] used part of the prayer (vv. 31-32) in an attempt to identify the situation lying behind some of the individual laments in the Psalter, the psalms he called 'the prayers of the accused'. If this approach is at all valid, then the prayer as a whole will provide a setting for the prayers of the Old Testament, most of which have come down to us as isolated psalms, leaving us to guess at their *Sitz im Leben*.

The prayer is generally regarded as a Deuteronomistic composition. The question of its historical worth hardly concerns us: it does not matter whether Solomon prayed such a prayer, provided that it reflects Israelite practice during the period when the Psalms were being composed and used in the temple. More important is the need to allow for Deuteronomistic theological bias, for the doctrine that all obedience receives its reward, all disobedience its punishment, is more firmly held by the Deuteronomistic circle than by any other Old Testament writers. Yahweh 'keeps the covenant with his servants, who walk before him wholeheartedly, and acts loyally towards them' (1 Kgs 8.23). There can be no suggestion that God will not remain faithful to the covenant on his side; the only troubles contemplated are those which inevitably awaken a sense of guilt in the people of Israel. The catalogue of occasions for prayer is therefore deficient to the extent that circumstances that might possibly impugn the justice of God are omitted. Thus the person who is wrongfully accused is encouraged to pray, but not the person who has suffered an inexplicable reversal of fortune. The nation may pray *before* battle for the help of their God; but in famine, disease and defeat the only acceptable prayer is that which is accompanied by the confession of sin. The limitations of this catalogue of occasions for prayer must therefore be borne in mind.

---

1. H. Schmidt, *Das Gebet der Angeklagten im Alten Testament* (BZAW, 49; Giessen: Alfred Töpelmann, 1928).

Prayer as Appeal for Help

Nevertheless, it is interesting to note that each of the prayers mentioned here relates to some emergency.[2] Nothing is said about regular occasions for prayer or subjects for regular intercession. In later Judaism it would appear that prayer was offered regularly and frequently as a kind of tribute or act of homage,[3] and in the synagogue parts of the Psalter were regularly used in worship.[4] There is also evidence that Israelites of an earlier period prayed in a general way for the welfare of Jerusalem[5] and the safety and judicial wisdom of the king,[6] and even for the welfare of their country of exile.[7] But the prayers of Israel were not originally or predominantly regular devotions, but appeals to God in an emergency. Solomon's prayer, purporting as it does to catalogue the occasions when prayer would be made, provides some evidence of this, and an examination of the prayers actually recorded in the Old Testament confirms it.

The Psalter provides the great majority of the recorded prayers. Out of 147 psalms[8] over 80 relate to an emergency, that is, to a situation which has disturbed the normal pattern of good behaviour and prosperity which should mark the relations of Israel or the individual Israelite with Yahweh. In eleven of these[9] the emergency is past, and the psalmist is giving thanks for his or his people's deliverance by Yahweh. In five more[10] the mood of the psalm is one of complete confidence, although the danger still exists. In the remainder, although an expression of confidence or assurance may be reached at some point in the psalm, the note of urgent appeal is struck. Thus more than 60 psalms are in the nature of an appeal to God.[11] How large a proportion this is will be seen even more clearly when it is remembered that, of the psalms

2. Cf. 2 Chron. 20.9; and F. Heiler, *Prayer* (trans. S. McComb; London: Oxford University Press, 1932), p. 228: 'It is the concrete need of the moment which gives occasion for the prayer'.

3. Dan. 6.10; Acts 3.1; G.F. Moore, *Judaism in the First Centuries of the Christian Era: The Age of Tannaim* (3 vols.; Cambridge, MA: Harvard University Press, 1927–30), II, pp. 219-21.

4. W.O.E. Oesterley, *The Psalms* (London: SPCK, 1939), pp. 99-105.

5. Ps. 122.6-9.

6. Ps. 72.1, 15; Ezra 6.10.

7. Jer. 29.7.

8. Taking Pss. 9–10 and 42–43 as single psalms and noting that 14 = 53.

9. Pss. 18; 30; 32; 40; 66; 76; 92; 107; 116; 124; 138.

10. Pss. 11; 16; 23; 46; 73.

11. These include not only the psalms which Gunkel classified as individual laments (38-40 of them) and communal laments (seven of them), but also a number which he describes as royal psalms (Pss. 20; 144), liturgies (Pss. 12; 14 = 53; 60; 85), and psalms of mixed type (Pss. 9–10; 36; 40; 77; 89; 90; 94; 108; 123; 129; 137; 139).

which do not appear to relate to an emergency, some are not prayers at all,[12] others clearly belong to some special occasion, such as the king's accession[13] or a particular festival[14] or the bringing up of the ark to Jerusalem,[15] while a number of the hymns of praise which on the face of it are suitable for all occasions probably belonged to an enthronement festival.[16] Therefore the proportion of psalms composed for use in an emergency, as against those designed for regular acts of worship, is very high indeed. The Psalter gives considerable support to the contention that prayer in Israel was fundamentally understood as an appeal to God.

We should expect prayers outside the Psalter to fall into this category of pleas for help in time of crisis. Prayers that were not uttered in situations in some way exceptional would hardly be recorded in narrative and prophecy. The prayers attributed to Abraham,[17] Moses,[18] Joshua,[19] Hannah,[20] Samuel,[21] David,[22] Elijah,[23] Elisha,[24] Jehoshaphat,[25] Hezekiah,[26] Amos,[27] Jeremiah,[28] Ezekiel,[29] Jonah,[30] Habakkuk,[31] Ezra,[32] Daniel and others[33] are clear examples of the kind of prayer under discussion. The Psalter, on the other hand, since it

12. E.g. Pss. 1; 37; 45; 78.

13. Pss. 2; 21; 72; 110.

14. Ps. 81.

15. Ps. 132; cf. J.R. Porter, 'The Interpretation of 2 Samuel 6 and Psalm 132', *JTS* NS 5 (1954), pp. 161-75.

16. Pss. 47; 93; 95–99.

17. Gen. 18.16-33; 20.17.

18. Exod. 5.22-23; 15.25; 17.4; 32.11-13, 31-32; Num. 11.2, 11-15; 12.13; 14.13-19; 16.15, 22; 27.15-16; Deut. 9.26-29.

19. Josh. 7.7-9.

20. 1 Sam. 1.10.

21. 1 Sam. 7.9.

22. 2 Sam. 12.16; 24.10, 17.

23. 1 Kgs 17.20-21; 18.36-37; 19.4.

24. 2 Kgs 4.33; 6.17-18.

25. 2 Chron. 20.6-12.

26. Isa. 37.14-20 (= 2 Kgs 19.14-19); 38.10-20 (cf. 2 Kgs 20.2-3).

27. Amos 7.1-6.

28. Jer. 10.23-25; 11.18-20; 12.1-4; 14.7-9, 19-22; 15.15-18; 17.13-18; 18.19-23; 20.7-13 (or 7-18).

29. Ezek. 4.14; 9.8; 11.13; 20.49.

30. Jon. 2.1-9.

31. Hab. 1.2-4, 12-17.

32. Ezra 9.5-15.

33. Gen. 20.4-5 (Abimelech); 1 Kgs 13.6 (unnamed prophet); Neh. 9.5-37 (Levites); Joel 2.17 (priests); Zech. 1.12 (angel). Cf. Isa. 63.7–64.12; Lam. 5.1-22; Job 7.1-10, 12-21; 9.25-31; 10; 13.23-27; 14; 17.2-9 (or 2-16); 30.16-23; 1 Macc. 3.50-53; 4.30-33; Tob. 3.1-6; Jdt. 9.1-14; Add. Est. 13.8-17; 14.3-19; Bar. 2.11–3.8; Sir. 36.1-22; *Prayer of AzariaH* 2-22; *Prayer of Manasseh; 3 Macc.* 2.1-20; 6.1-15.

ultimately became 'the hymn book of the second temple' and of the synagogue, might be expected to include as much material as possible which was suitable for regular and general use.

Akkadian prayers are likewise predominantly appeals for help in a specific situation rather than petitions for general benefits. Apart from prayers preserved in inscriptions, which ask for the general welfare of the king concerned,[34] nearly all prayers ask for help in some emergency. The common *šu-illa*, or 'prayer with uplifted hands', for example, always contains a complaint and a petition for deliverance.[35] The same characteristic may be noticed in such Hittite prayers as we have.[36] It is less obvious in Sumerian and Egyptian prayers: Sumerian poetry consists chiefly of official cult lyrics,[37] and was supplemented in use by the more popular Akkadian prayers; many Egyptian prayers are taken from the walls of tombs, and therefore understandably contain rather more general petitions for the welfare of the dead.[38]

Criteria for a Secular Analogy

We may now discuss the conditions that a secular analogy to such prayers would have to satisfy. There would seem to be four of these:

(1)   it must be an appeal for help;
(2)   it must be addressed to a superior from an inferior;
(3)   it must preferably come from Israel itself or from a society known to have influenced Israel;
(4)   it must come from a period not too distant in time from that in which most of the Old Testament prayers were composed.

The first three of these conditions are self-evident. So indeed is the fourth, but further discussion is necessary because there have been widely divergent views about the date of the psalms, and it cannot be claimed even now that complete certainty or unanimity has been reached. The fact that the Mesopotamian psalms have been discovered in the orderly excavation of ancient sites, and that in some cases they include the names of known historical figures, means that they, or at least the copies, can be fairly accurately dated. The fact that the biblical psalms have been handed down together as part of the scriptures means that no such evidence for their dating exists. The tradition preserved in the psalm titles, that many of the psalms are to be associated with David, is of doubtful antiquity and cannot be accepted uncritically, without confirmatory evidence. However, a Maccabaean dating for the psalms now

34. *SAHG* B Nos. 24-38; *HPD*, pp. 504-26.
35. *SAHG* B Nos. 40-81; *HPD*, pp. 269-346.
36. *CTH* 371-89; *ANET*, pp. 393-401.
37. *SAHG*, p. 18; *HPD*, p. 18.
38. Barucq, *L'expression*, p. 24.

seems out of the question.[39] Sirach (Prologue and 47.8; c.190 BCE) knew a threefold canon and the tradition associating the psalms with David; 1 Maccabees (7.16-17; late second century BCE) quotes Ps. 79.2-3 as scripture; there is a fragmentary second century BCE copy of the Psalms at Qumran (4QPsa); and the psalms composed by the Qumran community are very different in language, mood and theology from the biblical psalms, while the meter and parallelism of biblical poetry have largely disappeared.[40] It is now widely held that most of the psalms are pre-exilic, and a number of different grounds are given for this. References to the king are most naturally explained as having originated during the time when Israel and/or Judah actually had a king.[41] The use by the prophets of the hymn style or the lament style, in contrast to their normal oracular style, bears witness to the existence of a flourishing psalmody.[42] Similarly, the exiles in Babylon knew the 'songs of Zion' which they were unwilling to sing (Ps. 137.3-4).[43] Comparison with the Ugaritic literature shows many points of resemblance in vocabulary, style and ideas, and the most likely time for Canaanite influence to have been exercised would have been in the early days of the monarchy, when a Jebusite cultus in Jerusalem was probably absorbed into the worship of Yahweh.[44] The laments in the Psalter stand midway in point of length, elaboration and balance between the brief laments attributed to the Judges period (Josh. 7.7-9; Judg. 6.22; 15.18; 21.3) and the penitential laments of the Maccabaean period and later.[45] The lack of precise historical allusions still makes it impossible to date more than a very few individual psalms even to their century. Psalm 137 certainly belongs to the exile, but other communal laments (Pss. 44; 74; 79) can plausibly be assigned to any of a number of periods of national distress. Nevertheless, the considerations mentioned make it almost certain that most of the psalms, and in particular the individual laments, are pre-exilic.

Secular analogies to the prayers in the Psalter should ideally come from Israel itself. Gerstenberger, in *Der bittende Mensch*, precedes his analysis of the Babylonian exorcism prayers with a section on 'everyday requests' in

---

39. G. Fohrer, *Introduction to the Old Testament* (London: SPCK, 1970), p. 284; P.R. Ackroyd, 'Criteria for the Maccabean Dating of Old Testament Literature', *VT* 3 (1952), pp. 113-32; *idem, Exile and Restoration* (London: SCM Press), p. 45; Mowinckel, *Psalms*, II, pp. 198-99.

40. F.M. Cross, *The Ancient Library of Qumran* (London: Gerald Duckworth, 1958), pp. 122-23.

41. O. Eissfeldt, *The Old Testament: An Introduction* (Oxford: Basil Blackwell, 1965), p. 103; Johnson, 'The Psalms', pp. 167-68.

42. Gunkel and Begrich, *Einleitung*, §12; Mowinckel, *Psalms*, II, pp. 146-58.

43. Johnson, 'The Psalms', p. 195.

44. Mowinckel, *Psalms*, II, pp. 150, 187-89.

45. Westermann, 'Struktur', pp. 46-50, 66-72 = *Forschung*, pp. 268-72, 291-96; *Praise and Lament*, pp. 168-72, 198-207.

Israel, examining some 250 passages from the earlier narrative books of the Hebrew Bible (pp. 17-63). Some analogies between such requests and the individual complaint psalms are drawn out—the structures of both are compared (p. 127)—but not as fully or systematically as one might wish. By no means all these passages are urgent appeals for help—they include invitations to accept hospitality, proposals for mutual help and co-operation and requests for blessings—and the parties may be of equal status. The examples which are clearly appeals for help from an inferior to a superior are relatively few.[46] Archaeology has not produced many texts of Israelite provenance to supplement these: the Lachish letters alone come to mind.[47] It is therefore necessary to look further afield.

Ancient Near Eastern Letters

The most important source is that provided by *letters*. Speeches, oral appeals from one person to another, would be preferable, but understandably these are rarely recorded.[48] Indeed, the Egyptian Eighteenth Dynasty inscription from the tomb of Rekhmire, which details the duties of the vizier, insists that all petitions should be made in writing and not orally.[49] The disadvantages of using letters are not serious. Care was taken that they should not be tampered with and that they should arrive promptly,

> (Let the scribe) write it down from his dictation, let it be sealed with the cross-shaped (stamp) seal, and let Ahu-dur-enši, the cohort commander of the crown prince, quickly bring it to me by express delivery (ABL 434 [SAA 16, No. 148], ll. R 9-17).[50]

In the earliest period (nineteenth–eighteenth centuries BCE) they appear to be composed as if they were to be delivered verbally by a messenger, as the opening formula indicates:

> To Yahdun-Lîm say this: Thus (says) Abî-Samar (ARM, I, 1; *DEPM*, I, pp. 481-82 [No. 305]).

---

46. Josh. 10.6; 1 Sam. 7.8; 12.19; 19.4-5; 22.3; 24.9-15; 25.23-31; 26.18-20; 27.5; 2 Sam. 14.4-7, 32; 19.18-20, 26-28; 20.18-19; 1 Kgs 1.15-21; 18.9-14; 2 Kgs 4.27-28; 6.5, 26-29; 16.7; 18.14.

47. Lachish Letters 3 and 4. D. Pardee, *Handbook of Ancient Hebrew Letters* (SBL Sources for Biblical Study, 15; Chico, CA: Scholars Press, 1982), pp. 81-95.

48. The most notable examples are the appeals of captives recorded in the inscriptions of Ramesses III: see W.F. Edgerton and J.A. Wilson, *Historical Records of Ramses III* (Oriental Institute of the University of Chicago: Studies in Ancient Oriental Civilisation 12; Chicago: University of Chicago Press, 1936), pp. 3, 15, 45-46, etc.

49. *ARE*, II, §691.

50. Delivery would probably be by mule; cf. *Prosopography*, 1/I A, *s.v.* Ahu-dur-enši §1.

A king like Šamši-Addu evidently had his letters read aloud to him:

> I have listened to the messages you have sent me (ARM, I, 6; *DEPM,* II, pp. 342-44 [No. 641]; Oppenheim, *Letters,* No. 35).[51]

Similarly, in a rather fragmentary letter, Esarhaddon, replying to a complaint that he has ignored a letter sent to him:

> As [to what you wrote to me]: 'You did not read [nor open the letter] which [I sent] to you'. How [would] I [not do] thi[s]? When a letter which [you send to me comes] to [my re]porter, [*he per*]*sonally* [*opens*] the let[ter] and [makes me hear] its [infor]mation. [Wh]y [should I read] a letter? I take care of myself. (When) I see [a letter], I do not open it nor r[ead it]. (CT 53 391 [SAA 16, No. 6], ll. 1-9).

The petitioner might appeal to the scribe whose duty it was to read the letter. Thus Nabû-zer-ketti-lešir:

> Whoever you are, O scribe, who are reading (this letter), do not hide it from the king, your lord! Speak for me before the king, so Bel (and) Nabû may speak for you before the king (ABL 1250 [SAA 16, No. 32], ll. 17-22).

The chief importance of the written message was that it verified the verbal message, as a passage from the Hittite treaty between Tudhaliyas II and Šunaššura of Kissuwatna (c. 1400 BCE) shows:

> Furthermore: In regard to a tablet which I, My Majesty, send you—a tablet upon which words have been set down—and the words <of> the messenger, which he speaks orally to you—if the words of the messenger are in agreement with the words of the tablet, trust that messenger, O Sunaššura. But if the words of the speech of the messenger are not in agreement with the words of the tablet, you, Sunaššura, shall certainly not trust the messenger and shall certainly not take to heart the evil content of that report of his. Again: if the Sun sends you a letter (tablet), in which letter the (record) of a matter has been put down, and the messenger reports (verbally) to you about the matter which he has brought to you: if the words of the messenger agree with the wording of the letter, then you, Sunaššura, are to trust (believe) him. But if the words which you have from the mouth of the messenger do not correspond with the words of the letter, Sunaššura, you are not to trust him; and you shall surely not take any harm in your heart over these words (*CTH* 41; *HDT,* No. 2, §59, p. 24).

Kept as a record, it could also be valuable proof of a vassal's loyalty, as Rib-Hadda of Byblos points out to the pharaoh in one of the Amarna letters:

> May the king inspect the tablets of his father's house for the time when the ruler in Gubla was not a loyal servant (EA 74, ll. 10-12).

---

51. A.L. Oppenheim, *Letters from Mesopotamia* (Chicago: University of Chicago Press, 1967). Cf. ARM XXVI.148, ll. 5-9 (*AEM,* p. 313).

The letters of the ancient Near East cover many aspects of international diplomacy, administration, law, business and private life. (Translations of 150 representative Akkadian letters are given in Oppenheim's *Letters*.) Not all therefore are appeals for help, but many are. Not all are from inferiors to superiors, but even the replies of superiors sometimes allow the correspondent's appeal to be reconstructed, sometimes even quote it, as in a letter from Suppululiumaš, the Hittite king, to Niqmaddu, king of Ugarit:

> Niqmaddu, king of the land of Ugarit, turned to Šuppuliliumaš, Great King, writing: 'May our Majesty, Great King, my lord, save me from the hand of my enemy. I am the subject of Your Majesty, Great King, my lord. To my lord's enemy I am hostile, [and] with my lord's friend I am at peace. The kings are oppressing (?) me' (*CTH* 46; *HDT*, No. 4, §2, p. 35).

Letters may lack the immediacy of direct oral address, but they record in detail the description of events, the enquiries, the promises, the explanations, the arguments used. In the completeness of their record, therefore, they are very suitable for comparison with the biblical prayers.

We have still to determine which collections of letters are most relevant to our purpose. The letters come from widely separated places and periods. There are letters from Elam, Anatolia, Syria and Egypt, as well as from many sites in Mesopotamia. The earliest letters in Oppenheim's selection were written at the end of the third millennium BCE, and the latest from just before the conquests of Alexander the Great in the fourth century BCE. The most important collections are as follows:

(1)   the Mari letters, from the nineteenth and eighteenth centuries BCE;[52]

(2)   the Alalakh tablets of the eighteenth and fifteenth centuries BCE;[53]

(3)   the Amarna letters, from the early fourteenth century BCE;[54]

---

52.   A. Parrot and G. Dossin (eds.), *Archives royales de Mari* (28 vols.; I–IX, Paris: Imprimerie Nationale, 1950–60; X–XXI, Paris: P. Geuthner, 1963–83; XXII–XXVIII, Paris: Éditions Recherche sur les Civilisations, 1948–98); J-M. Durand, *Les documents épistolaires du palais de Mari* (Littératures anciennes du Proche-Orient, 16-18; Paris: Les Éditions du Cerf; I, 1997; II, 1998; III, 2000; cited as *DEPM*); *idem*, *Archives Épistolaires de Mari*, I/1 and D. Churpin, F. Joannès, S. Lackenbacher and B. Lafont, *Archives Épistolaires de Mari*, I/2 (Archives royales de Mari, XXVI; Paris: Editions Recherche sur les Civilisations, 1988; cited as *AEM*).

53.   D.J. Wiseman, *The Alalakh Tablets* (Occasional Publications of the British Institute of Archaeology in Ankara, 2; London: British Institute of Archaeology at Ankara, 1953).

54.   J.A. Knudtzon, *Die El-Amarna Tafeln* (Vorderasiatische Bibliothek, 2; 2 vols.; Leipzig: J.C. Hinrichs, 1907–15); S.A.B. Mercer, *The Tell el-Amarna Tablets* (2 vols.; Toronto: Macmillan, 1939); A.F. Rainey, *El Amarna Tablets 359–379* (AOAT, 8; Neukirchen–Vluyn: Neukirchener Verlag, 1978); W.L. Moran, *The Amarna Letters* (Baltimore: The John Hopkins University Press, 1992) (cited as EA).

(4) letters from Ugarit, from the fourteenth to the twelfth centuries BCE;[55]

(5) Hittite letters from Bogazköy, from the thirteenth century BCE;[56]

(6) Assyrian letters from Nimrud, from the second half of the eighth century BCE;[57]

(7) Assyrian letters from Nineveh, from the eighth and seventh centuries BCE.[58]

(1) Many letters from Mari satisfy the first two conditions: they are appeals for help, and they are addressed by inferiors to superiors. There are letters from the neighbouring king Abi-Samar to Yahdun-Lim, king of Mari, when both were being threatened by Šamši-Addu of Assyria. After the latter's conquest of the city, there are letters between him and his son and viceroy at Mari, Yasmah-Addu. There is a large number of letters to Yasmah-Addu and his successor Zimri-Lim from officials in the towns and districts around

---

55. *Mission de Ras Shamra* VI and IX = C.F.A. Schaeffer (ed.), *Le palais royal d'Ugarit* III and IV (Paris: Imprimerie Nationale, 1955), *Mission de Ras Shamra* XVI = J. Nougayrol *et al.*, *Ugaritica* V (Paris: Imprimerie Naitionale, 1968) (cited as RS).

56. G. Beckman, *Hittite Diplomatic Texts* (SBL Writings from the Ancient World, 7; Atlanta: Scholars Press, 2nd edn, 1999), pp. 125-52 (cited as *HDT*).

57. H.W.F. Saggs, *The Nimrud Letters 1952* (Cuneiform Texts from Nimrud, 5; British School of Archaeology in Iraq, 2001). Many of the letters were previously published in *Iraq* 17 (1955), pp. 21-56; 18 (1956), pp. 40-56; 20 (1958), pp. 182-212; 21 (1959), pp. 158-79; 25 (1963), pp. 70-80; 27 (1965), pp. 17-32; 28 (1966), pp. 177-91; 36 (1974), pp. 199-221 (cited as ND).

58. R.F. Harper, *Assyrian and Babylonian Letters* (14 vols.; London: British Museum; Chicago: University of Chicago Press, 1892–1914) (cited as ABL); L. Waterman, *Royal Correspondence of the Assyrian Empire* (University of Michigan Studies, Humanistic Series, 17-20; Ann Arbor: University of Michigan Press, 1930–36); S. Parpola, *Letters from Assyrian Scholars to the Kings Esarhaddon and Assurbanipal* (AOAT, 5; Neukirchen–Vluyn: Neukirchener Verlag, I [Texts], 1970; II [Commentary and Appendices], 1983) (cited as *LAS*); S. Parpola, *The Correspondence of Sargon II. I. Letters from Assyria and the West* (SAA, 1; Helsinki: Helsinki University Press, 1987) (cited as SAA 1); G.B. Lanfranchi and S. Parpola, *The Correspondence of Sargon II. II. Letters from the Northern and Northeastern Provinces* (SAA, 5; Helsinki: Helsinki University Press, 1990) (cited as SAA 5); S. Parpola, *Letters from Assyrian and Babylonian Scholars* (SAA, 10; Helsinki: Helsinki University Press, 1993) (cited as SAA 10); S.W. Cole and P. Machinist, *Letters from Priests to the Kings Esarhaddon and Assurbanipal* (SAA, 13; Helsinki: Helsinki University Press, 1998) (cited as SAA 13); M. Luukko and G. Van Buylaere, *The Political Correspondence of Esarhaddon* (SAA, 16; Helsinki: Helsinki University Press, 2002) (cited as SAA 16); M. Dietrich, *The Neo-Babylonian Correspondence of Sargon and Sennacherib* (SAA, 17; Helsinki: Helsinki University Press, 2003) (cited as SAA 17); F.S. Reynolds, *The Babylonian Correspondence of Esarhaddon and Letters to Assurbanipal and Sin-šarru-iškun from Northern and Central Babylonia* (SAA, 18; Helsinki: Helsinki University Press, 2003) (cited as SAA 18).

Mari, and particularly from Kibri-Dagan, Zimri-Lim's governor in Terqa.[59] Abi-Samar appeals to Yahdun-Lim for protection; Yasmah-Addu appeals to Šamši-Addu for more troops; women complain that they are being detained or maligned; Kibri-Dagan appeals for help in building a canal; and so on.[60] But do the Mari letters satisfy the other conditions? Did Mari influence Israel at a time sufficiently near to the composition of the psalms? Parallels between Mari and the Old Testament have frequently been pointed out.[61] These parallels, understandably enough, have been chiefly with the patriarchal narratives. But interest has also been shown in the existence at Mari of functionaries resembling the Old Testament prophets,[62] who do not appear, as far as we know, until a period much later than that of the patriarchs. Admittedly the evidence Mari provides for the antecedents of Hebrew prophecy is important chiefly because other evidence, nearer in place and time, is lacking. In relation to our own subject, we may say that Mari is too remote to be of primary importance. Nevertheless the resemblances in the field of prophecy suggest that use may be made of parallels from Mari when they are particularly striking. This will not imply any direct influence of Mari on the culture of the Old Testament, but will simply indicate the antiquity and diffusion of the letter writing tradition.

(2) The Alalakh tablets provide many points of comparison with the Old Testament, again particularly with the patriarchal period,[63] but only one or two letters can be described as appeals for help. Other documents provide incidental illustrations of particular points.

(3) The Amarna letters provide what are almost paradigm cases of the material we are looking for. These were written during the early fourteenth century BCE, to Amenophis III and Amenophis IV (Akhenaten), from their vassals and officials in Syria and Palestine.[64] Thus many of the letters were written on the soil of Palestine itself, and presumably the same tradition of letter writing would have persisted up to the time of the Israelite settlement,

59. See J. Laessøe, *People of Ancient Assyria* (London: Routledge & Kegan Paul, 1963), p. 44.

60. ARM, I, 1, 22; II, 66, 113, 115; III, 3 (*DEPM*, I, p. 481 [No. 305]; II, p. 55 [No. 476]; III, pp. 479-80 [No. 1251]; III, p. 468 [No. 1244]; III, pp. 438-39 [No. 1226]; II, p. 601 [No. 798]).

61. A. Parrot, 'Mari', in *AOTS*), pp. 136-44; G.E. Wright, *Biblical Archaeology* (London: Gerald Duckworth, 1956), pp. 41-42, 96-97; G.E. Mendenhall, 'Mari', in Freedman and Campbell (eds.), *Biblical Archaeology Reader 2*, pp. 3-20.

62. M. Noth, *The Laws in the Pentateuch and Other Studies* (Edinburgh: Oliver & Boyd, 1966), pp. 179-93.

63. D.J. Wiseman, 'Alalakh', in *AOTS*, pp. 119-35.

64. W.F. Albright, 'The Amarna Letters from Palestine', in CAH, II.2, pp. 98-116 (98-102).

just as the religious traditions embodied in the Ugaritic myths of the fourteenth century are presumed to have persisted in Canaan and influenced the religious literature of Israel. It is highly likely that we have here a style with which Israel became acquainted, especially if Israelite kingship was at all modelled on Canaanite kingship, as the description in 1 Sam. 8.11-18 may well imply.[65] A very high proportion of the Amarna letters consists of appeals for help, because they were written at a time when Egypt's hold on Syria-Palestine was weakening, and the pharaoh's subordinates were being threatened both by each other and by the marauding Habiru.[66] The note of urgent appeal is well marked in this letter to the pharaoh from Rib-Hadda, the pharaoh's agent in Gubla (Byblos):

> Rib-Hadda says to his lord, king of all countries, Great King: May the Lady of Gubla grant power to the king, my lord. I fall at the feet of my lord, my Sun, seven times and seven times. May the king, my lord, know that Gubla, the loyal maidservant of the king, is safe and sound. The war, however, of the 'Apiru forces against me is extremely severe, and so may the king, my lord, not neglect Sumur lest everyone be joined to the 'Apiru forces. Through the king's commissioner who is in Sumur, Gubla is alive. Pahamnata, the commissioner of the king who is in Sumur, knows the straits that Gubla is in. It is from the land of Yarimuta that we have acquired provisions. The war against us is extremely severe, and so may the king not neglect his cities (EA 68).

(4) The Amarna letters no longer stand alone as evidence for the letter writing of that area and that period. One of the Amarna letters[67] was written by Ammištamru, king of Ugarit, c. 1400 BCE, and there are references to Ugarit in the letters of its neighbours.[68] The excavations at Ras Shamra (Ugarit) itself have now produced some 170 letters in Akkadian cuneiform and 85 in alphabetic cuneiform.[69] These letters were written in the fourteenth and thirteenth centuries BCE, and show that in the reign of Niqmaddu II Ugarit became tributary to the Hittite kingdom, and remained so until the destruction of the city by the 'sea peoples' early in the twelfth century.[70] The correspondence of the kings of Ugarit was frequently with the Hittite overlord or

---

65. I. Mendelsohn, 'Samuel's Denunciation of Kingship in the Light of the Akkadian Documents from Ugarit', *BASOR* 143 (1956), pp. 17-22.

66. Albright, 'Amarna Letters', pp. 110-12.

67. EA 45; see W.F. Albright, 'An Unrecognised Amarna Letter from Ugarit', *BASOR* 95 (1944), pp. 30-33.

68. EA 89, l. 51; 98, l. 9; 126, l. 6; 151, l. 55; cf. also a letter of Amenophis III: EA 1, l. 39.

69. Nougayrol *et al.*, *Ugaritica* V, pp. 41, 66; J.-L. Cunchillos (ed.), *Textes Ugaritiques*. II. *Correspondance: Introduction, traduction, commentaire* (Paris: Cerf, 1989), p. 243.

70. M. Drower, 'Ugarit in the Fourteenth and Thirteenth Centuries BC', in CAH, II.2, pp. 130-48 (137-48).

with neighbouring kings of equal rank: there are fewer letters from officials and none from vassals. Also, not many of the letters could be described as appeals for help. Nevertheless, there are some examples, such as this letter from the prefect of Qadeš:

> To the king of Ugarit, my master, say: Thus (says) Padiya, prefect of Qadeš, [y]our ser[vant:] At the feet of my master, from afar, twice seven times I fall down. [As for me](?), at Qadeš, (I am) your servant. The[refore,] m[ay m]y mas[ter] g[i]ve his servant [advi]ce(?)! Before the great men, my brothers, I have declared: 'The king of Ugarit is my master'. May my master therefore prove his favour to his servant! And may my master not abandon his servant! So then, all that my master asks of his servant I will give my master. But, as to (my own) request, I hope my master has sent me…[the request is repeated in detail]. Now I have declared to my brothers: 'It is a great king who has taken (me) (into his service) and he shows me favour'. So then, may my master not put me to shame before my brothers. What my master gives to his servant, may he give (truly)! (RS 20.16, ll. 1-19, 38-44)

(5) The fact that Ugarit was so directly under Hittite influence at this period makes the Hittite letters from Bogazköy of the thirteenth century BCE relevant, just as the Hittite treaties are relevant to the study of the Old Testament covenants. In fact, however, there is no letter that is actually an appeal for help from a vassal or official. Nevertheless, occasional features of the common letter writing tradition will be illustrated from Hittite material.

(6) and (7) The letters from the late Assyrian period found at Nimrud and Nineveh are second only in importance to the Amarna letters. Most of them are letters from royal officials or vassals to the Assyrian kings Tiglath-pileser III, Shalmaneser V and Sargon II (Nimrud) and Esarhaddon and Aššurbanipal (Nineveh). The letters are an invaluable source for the history of the reigns of the last two kings,[71] and they also include a number of appeals for help.

The royal officials had to contend with revolts by conquered peoples and inroads by foreign tribes, as well as maintain the routine administration of the provinces. They also frequently had to defend themselves against accusations and complaints.[72] The following letter from an official in Nippur illustrates some of the problems that had to be faced:

> The king knows that I am very sick. Had I not been sick, I would have gone to the king to inquire about his health. So I am sending herewith my brother Belusatu and ten well-born citizens of Nippur to inquire about the health of Your Majesty.
>
> The king well knows that people hate us everywhere on account of our allegiance to Assyria. We are not safe anywhere; wherever we might go we would be killed. People say: 'Why did you submit to Assyria?' We have now

---

71. See A.T. Olmstead, *History of Assyria* (New York: Charles Schribner's Sons, 1923).

72. Waterman, *Royal Correspondence*, IV, pp. 22-23.

locked our gates tight and do not even go out of town into the… We are still
doing our duty for the king; the envoy and the officials whom the king has sent
here have seen all this and can tell the king about it. But the king must not
abandon us to the others! We have no water and are in danger of dying for
lack of water. The king your father wanted to give us the water rights for the
Banitu-canal under this condition: 'Dig an outlet from the Banitu-canal toward
Nippur'. [The…], however, refused us the water. The king should now send an
order to Ubaru, the commander of Babylon, to grant us an outlet from the
Banitu-canal so that we can drink water with them from it and not have to
desert the king on account of lack of water. They must not say everywhere:
'These are the inhabitants of Nippur who submitted to Assyria—and when they
became sick and tired of the lack of water they deserted' (ABL 327, ll. 5-R22;
Oppenheim, *Letters*, No. 121).

These Assyrian letters were all written at the time when Assyria's influence
on Israel and Judah was at its maximum. War and the threat of war dissemi-
nated Assyrian culture in the west.[73] The kings of Israel and Judah paid tribute and imported Assyrian cults.[74] People from the Assyrian empire were
settled in Samaria.[75] Officials demanding surrender appeared at the gates of
Jerusalem and harangued its citizens.[76] Hezekiah received letters, not only
from the king of Assyria,[77] but also from the Chaldaean leader Merodach-
baladan (Marduk-apla-idinna), who was in revolt against Assyria.[78] Thus we
know that letters of the type found at Nimrud and Nineveh were received at
Jerusalem. If any of the psalms were composed in this period—and there is a
tradition of some literary activity in the reign of Hezekiah[79]—then it is quite
possible that Assyrian official procedure and correspondence exercised an
indirect, perhaps quite unconscious, influence upon their content.

Thus connections or parallels with the Old Testament have already been
noticed in all these major collections of letters. In two cases, those of the
Amarna letters and the Assyrian letters, there is a strong possibility that the
traditions they represent were actually known to Israel. It is also important to
notice that the collections themselves are evidence that a common letter writing tradition existed in the ancient Near East and persisted for over a thousand
years. The differences in style and content are not more striking than the
resemblances. For one thing, although the letters come from widely separated

---

73. Widengren, *Psalms of Lamentation*, p. 4.
74. 2 Kgs 15.19-20; 16.7-8, 10-18; 18.14-16; 21.5.
75. 2 Kgs 17.24-28.
76. 2 Kgs 18.17-37 = Isa. 36.2-22. On the appeal to the populace as a deliberate Assyrian policy, see John S. Holladay, Jr, 'Assyrian Statecraft and the Prophets of Israel', *HTR*
63 (1970), pp. 29-51.
77. 2 Kgs 19.8-14 = Isa. 37.8-14.
78. 2 Kgs 20.12 = Isa. 39.1.
79. Prov. 25.1; Isa. 38.9-20.

periods and regions, the vast majority of them are in Akkadian cuneiform, which remained the *lingua franca* of the ancient Near East for as long a time as Latin was the *lingua franca* of Western Christendom. There are other examples of the early spread of Akkadian influence in the countries bordering on the Mediterranean,[80] but none so remarkable as the fact that the Hittite and Egyptian kings should correspond in Akkadian[81] or that the pharaoh's vassals and officials in Syria and Palestine should report to him in Akkadian.

Certain formulas and stylistic features recur. A king is always addressed in the third person ('May my lord send me an answer to my letter'). In Old Babylonian, Assyrian and Neo-Babylonian letters it is common to open with a wish that the gods may protect the addressee; this feature appears also in letters from Ugarit, but it is rare in the Mari and Amarna letters. Correspondents from Mari onwards frequently give an assurance that all is well with them: this is particularly noticeable in letters from the pharaoh and the Assyrian king. The formula of homage used by officials and vassals in the Amarna letters ('Seven times and again seven times I prostrate myself at the feet of the king, my lord, and my sun') reappears only slightly altered in letters to the king of Ugarit from his officials ('Twice seven times I prostrate myself before my lord, even from afar'). This continuity extends also to the motifs and arguments used in the letters, as the rest of this study will illustrate.

It is clear from the evidence of a common epistolary tradition that it would be pedantic to look only for the influence of this collection of letters or that on the Old Testament. What the letters show above all is that there was an accepted way of writing letters in the ancient Near East. Everywhere letters had the same functions, covered the same subjects, used the same arguments and adopted much the same style. Local variations there were bound to be, but these did not disturb the underlying continuity.

What Kind of Parallel?

We may now ask what kind of parallel may be expected between the letters and the biblical prayers. Certainly not any that would imply direct literary dependence. Letters are generally read only by those to whom they are addressed: they do not obtain the same currency as stories, poems, hymns for cultic use, inscriptions, law codes and treaties. Therefore it is extremely unlikely that any psalmist read any of the letters known to us. It is only the letter writing tradition in general which could have had any influence on the psalmists, not any extant letter.

---

80. R. Labat, 'Le rayonnement de la langue et de l'écriture akkadiennes du deuxième millénaire avant notre ère', *Syria* 39 (1962), pp. 1-27; Wiseman, *Alalakh Tablets*, pp. 180-87; Widengren, *Psalms of Lamentation*, pp. 11-12.
81. EA 17-21; 23; 24; 27-29; 41.

Nor will there be any close resemblance in form between the letters and the biblical prayers. Most of the latter are poetical in form, keeping more or less strictly to a metrical pattern and employing parallelism. Although passages of a rhythmical or strophic pattern have been noted in the Amarna letters,[82] this is not a general feature of the letters; they are prose documents.

Some types of Akkadian psalm follow a fairly rigid order of motifs.[83] Both the Israelite psalms and secular letters have a much freer structure, but it is unlikely that the letters exercised any influence over the psalms in this respect.

The letters are full of names, figures and facts, as the psalms are not. The contrast is partly due to the fact that the psalms, even if composed for particular occasions, were adapted for repeated use in an indefinite number of similar situations.[84] But it is also true that prayer to a god lacks the concreteness of an appeal to 'a living and capricious master'.[85] The same contrast may be seen between hymns to a king and hymns to a deity both in Egypt and in Mesopotamia: the former have to 'take cognisance of actual achievements, current fashions, and ideals', whereas the religious hymns use 'tradition-bound terms'.[86] On the other hand, the psalms describe conditions of danger with varied imagery, whereas the letters are more matter-of-fact. In the letters, as we have seen, vassals normally address the king in the third person; in the psalms direct address is more usual, and where the third person address occurs, it may reflect the usage of letters and courtly speech.[87]

The analogy between the letters and the prayers lies much more in content than in style, though certain expressions, particularly expressions of dependence, are common to both.[88] Appeal to God and appeal to a king or other superior were essentially regarded as the same kind of activity.[89] Virtually the same arguments might be used, for God and king would be moved in much the same way.

The parallel between the two activities was consciously recognised. Psalm 123 makes the comparison very plainly, as G.R. Castellino has noted: 'The

82. See Appendix.
83. E.g. the *šu-illa*.
84. Widengren, *Psalms of Lamentation*, p. 155.
85. Oppenheim, *Letters*, p. 29.
86. Oppenheim, *Letters*, p. 29; cf. Barucq, *L'expression*, p. 307.
87. W.W. Hallo, 'Individual Prayer in Sumerian: The Continuity of a Tradition', in *idem* (ed.), *Essays in Memory of E.A. Speiser* (American Oriental Series, 53; New Haven: American Oriental Society, 1968 [= *JAOS* 88/1]), pp. 71-89 (80); cf. Widengren, *Psalms of Lamentation*, p. 36.
88. See Chapter 8.
89. Cf. Richard J. Clifford, *Psalms 1–72* (Abingdon Old Testament Commentaries; Nashville: Abingdon Press, 2002), p. 47: 'In psalms of supplication the relationship between the psalmist and God often seems to be modelled after the social relationship of a powerful patron and a dependent client'.

sense of a more intimate attachment to God together with the attitude of obsequiousness and devotion is expressed in Ps. 123.2 by means of a comparison, of frequent use in social and religious contexts drawn from the relation of master and slave'.[90]

> See, as the eyes of servants
> Look to the hand of their masters,
> And as the eyes of a servant-girl
> Look to the hand of her mistress,
> So our eyes look to Yahweh our God
> Until he has mercy on us (Ps. 123.2).

One of the Hittite 'Plague Prayers of Mursilis II' is equally explicit:

> The bird takes refuge in (its) nest, and the nest saves its life. Again, if anything becomes too much for a servant, he appeals to his lord,. His lord hears him and takes pity on him. Whatever has become too much for him he sets right for him. Again: if the servant has incurred a guilt, but confesses his guilt to his lord, his lord may do with him whatever he pleases. But because (the servant) has confessed his guilt to his lord, his lord's soul is pacified, and his lord will not punish that servant. I have now confessed my father's sin (*CTH* 378; *ANET*, pp. 395-96; *CoS*, I.60 [Second Prayer, pp. 158-59]).

Mursilis' argument is that the Hittite storm god should act as a pacified master would, now that the king has done his best to discover the cause of his people's guilt and make restitution for it.

Letters to the Gods

Prayers sometimes even took the form of letters to the gods.[91] There are in Sumerian, in the early second millennium royal correspondence of Ur, Isin, Uruk and Larsa, a number of examples of letter prayers, which begin with the salutation 'To my god speak, thus says NN your servant'. Then follow complaint, protests, prayers, and formal reinforcements of the appeal. Two letters conclude by referring to '(my) letter which I have deposited before you'; this reflects the practice of leaving petitions in the temple, at the feet of the cult statue, which is attested by excavations. The concluding formulas are again borrowed from secular letters: 'May my king know it'; 'It is urgent'; 'Do not be negligent'; 'At the command of Enlil (my) eyes behold your face'; 'May

---

90. G.R. Castellino, 'Mesopotamian Parallels to some Passages in the Psalms', in H. Donner, R. Hanhart and R. Smend (eds.), *Beiträge zur Alttestamentlichen Theologie* (Festschrift W. Zimmerli; Göttingen: Vandenhoeck & Ruprecht, 1977), pp. 60-68 (67).

91. T. Jacobsen, 'Mesopotamia', in H. Frankfort, H.A. Frankfort, J.A. Wilson and T. Jacobsen, *Before Philosophy* (Harmondsworth: Penguin Books, 1949), pp. 137-234 (220).

the heart of my god (or king) be appeased'.[92] There are also Akkadian letter prayers from the Old Babylonian period: in one of them the suppliant asks his personal god to write to Marduk, the national god of Babylon.[93]

Originally these letter prayers were substitutes for votive objects. Eventually they in turn gave way to prose prayers and then to poetic laments.[94] Nevertheless the practice was revived occasionally. At Mari Yasmah-addu addressed a poignant letter to the god Nergal after being deprived of a male heir with the death of his son,[95] and Zimri-lim accompanied the offering of a golden vase to the river god with a letter imploring the god's protection.[96] The reports of Assyrian kings on victorious campaigns are letters to the gods in form, even if they were intended more for the ears of the citizens of Aššur.[97] And when Hezekiah received a threatening letter from Sennacherib, he thought it worthwhile to spread out the letter before Yahweh and invite him to read it as well as to hear it (2 Kgs 19.14, 16). We may take it that in the ancient Near East prayer and letter writing were not regarded as fundamentally dissimilar activities.

Connection between Treaty and Letter

The analogy between letters and prayers is related to that between treaty and covenant. At Bogazköy, Ugarit, Alalakh, Nimrud and Nineveh treaties have been found in the same archives as the letters we are considering. They represent different moments in the same relationship.

In the Hittite treaties, the right of vassals to appeal for help by letter is recognised, as the following clause from the treaty between Mursilis II and Tuppi-Teššup of Amurru shows:

> If some matter oppresses you, anyone should press you hard, Tuppi-Teššup, or someone revolts against you, and you write to the King of Hatti, then the King of Hatti will send infantry and chariotry to your aid (*CTH* 62; *HDT*, No. 8, §9, p. 61; cf. *ANET*, p. 204, §11).

Similarly, Hattusilis reminds Kadašman-Enlil II of Babylonia of the terms of a treaty previously made:

> If an enemy somehow arises against you, or some matter becomes troublesome for you, write to me so that I can come to your aid (*CTH* 172; *HDT*, No. 23, §4, p. 139).

92. Hallo, 'Individual Prayer', pp. 71-89; cf. for Egypt, G.R. Hughes, 'A Demotic Letter to Thoth', *JNES* 17 (1958), pp. 1-12.
93. Foster, *Before the Muses*, II.36-38, pp. 156-59.
94. Hallo, 'Individual Prayer', p. 75.
95. ARM I.3, ll. R24-29 (*DEPM*, III, p. 72 [No. 931]).
96. ARM XXVI.191 (*AEM*, I/1, p. 413).
97. Oppenheim, *Ancient Mesopotamia*, pp. 279-80.

In a letter to Niqmaddu II of Ugarit, proposing a treaty, the Hittite king, probably Šuppiluliumaš, encourages the vassal to appeal to him:

> And if all of the kings release whatever troops they have for an attack on your land, you, Niqmaddu, shall not fear them. Send your messenger to me immediately. Let him come! (*CTH* 45; *HDT*, No. 19, §4, p. 126).

The historical prologue to the treaty between Šuppiluliumaš and Tette of Nuhašši records an instance of such an appeal being made in the past:

> When (the king of Mitanni) oppressed (?) him, then Šarrupši sent his messenger to the King of Hatti, saying: 'I am the subject of the King of Hatti. Save me!' (*CTH* 53; *HDT*, No. 7, §1, p. 55).

This close connection between treaty and letter is also to be seen in Assyria. One of the most important discoveries at Nimrud has been that of the text of a treaty which Esarhaddon made with a number of his vassals in 672 BCE, requiring them to recognise the succession of Aššurbanipal to the throne of Assyria and that of his brother Šamaš-šumu-ukin to the throne of Babylonia.[98] It is clear, however, that this treaty is closely linked with the oath of loyalty that every one of the king's own officials had to take at the same time. Several letters from Nineveh refer to the taking of the oath in different localities.[99] In another, the well-known exorcist Adad-šumu-usur[100] refers to criticism of Esarhaddon's action in establishing the succession or, perhaps, in dividing it, but himself applauds it.[101] Two more are in fact excerpts from the oath as it was re-administered by Zakutu, the queen mother, the widow of Sennacherib, after the accession of Aššurbanipal.[102] Since the centralised territorial state was not the native and natural form of political organisation in Assyria, its smooth running depended entirely on the loyalty of the provincial governors and other officials.[103] The oath of allegiance was therefore the central feature of their relationship with the king. Correspondents sometimes show that they are aware of this. For example, an unknown official, reporting to Aššurbanipal on the action he has taken against rebels, says:

---

98. D.J. Wiseman, *The Vassal Treaties of Esarhaddon* (London: British School of Archaeology in Iraq, 1958 [= *Iraq* 20]), pp. 1-100; Laessøe, *People*, pp. 116-22.

99. ABL 33 (*LAS*, No. 2; SAA 10, No. 7); 202; 213; 384 (*LAS*, No. 3; SAA 10, No. 5); 386 (*LAS*, No. 1; SAA 10, No. 6).

100. On Adad-šumu-usur see K. Deller, 'Die Briefe der Adad-šumu-usur', in W. Röllig (ed.), Lišan mithurti. *FS Wolfram Freiherr von Soden zum 19.6.1968 gewidmet van Schülern und Mitarbeiten* (AOAT, 1; Kevelaer: Butzon & Bercker, 1969), pp. 45-64; *LAS*, I, pp. 88-125; II, pp. 101-58; *Prosopography*, 1/I A, *s.v.* Adad-šumu-usur, §5.

101. ABL 870 (*LAS*, No. 129; SAA 10, No. 185; Oppenheim, *Letters*, No. 98); and see *LAS*, II, p. 116.

102. ABL 1239; 1105.

103. Oppenheim, *Letters*, pp. 6-7; McCarthy, *Treaty and Covenant*, p. 88.

Lord of the watch and guardian of the oath (or, treaty) of the king, my lord, am
I (ABL 1341, l. 6).

A priest, reporting that he has made a royal proclamation public, adds:

I keep the king's treaty (ABL 555 [SAA 13, No. 45], ll. 7-8).

By the terms of the treaty of 672 BCE the vassals promised to protect
Aššurbanipal, to fight and die for him, to give him honest advice, to carry out
his commands, and not to plot or rise against him.[104] They were also expected
to tell the king about any plot or expression of public opinion that came to
their notice, a demand that is given prominent place in the oath imposed after
Aššurbanipal's accession.[105] Officials are well aware that this is their duty:

Is it not said in the treaty as follows: 'Anyone who hears something (but) does
not inform the king...'? (ABL 656 [*LAS*, No. 133; SAA 10, No. 199], ll. 18-
21; Wiseman, *Vassal Treaties*, p. 8).[106]

The king will also remind them of it, Aššurbanipal writes to Bel-ibni, governor of the Sealand:[107]

Just as somebody who loves the house of his master informs him about whatever he sees or hears, exactly so have you informed me (ABL 288, ll. 9-R4;
Oppenheim, *Letters*, No. 117).

Along with this duty went the right to make complaints and representations
direct to the king.[108] The words of Marduk-šarru-usur—

A servant who is in trouble petitions his masters. I am (now) in trouble and
petitioning the king, my lord (ABL 347 [SAA 16, No. 82], ll. 6-8)—

could have been echoed by many of those who wrote to the king.

Thus, both in Hittite diplomacy and in Assyrian statecraft, letters play an
important part in the relationships established by treaty or oath of loyalty.
References to oaths previously made or proposed are also found in letters
from Mari[109] and Semdara, another city which was tributary to Šamši-Addu

104. Wiseman, *Vassal Treaties*, col. i. 46-72, pp. 31-34; Laessøe, *People*, p. 118.

105. Wiseman, *Vassal Treaties*, col. i. 80-82, 120-22, 156-57, 170-71; Laessøe, *People*,
pp. 118-19; ABL 1105, ll. 7-16; 1239, ll. R2-25; Waterman, *Royal Correspondence*, IV,
p. 23; H.W.F. Saggs, *The Greatness that was Babylon* (London: Sidgwick & Jackson, 2nd
edn, 1988 [1962]), p. 106.

106. Cf. ABL 510; CT 53 938 (SAA 16, No. 61), l. 11. Parpola, *LAS*, II, p. 121, says
that this is not a 'direct quotation from the Vassal Treaties but rather a free rendering of its
main theme: the obligation of the treaty partners to keep the royal house informed on
everything'. Cf. Wiseman, *Vassal Treaties*, ll. 73-82: '(You swear) that you will neither
listen to not conceal any improper words...but will report these things'.

107. On Bel-ibni, see *Prosopography* I/II B-G, *s.v.*, §18, pp. 306-10.

108. Saggs, *Greatness*, p. 105.

109. Laessøe, *People*, pp. 41, 76.

of Aššur in the eighteenth century BCE.[110] There is no mention of an oath of loyalty in the Amarna letters, but correspondents express the same sense of being under obligation to the pharaoh and of having the right to appeal to him. The same kind of relationship is implicit.

Widengren says of the Akkadian prayers: 'God and his worshippers were here the two parties of a covenant, of a pact, by which both had assumed mutual obligations. As long as man fulfilled his obligations, he expected the god to fulfil his.'[111] While we may agree that worshippers expected their gods to behave *as if* they had entered into a treaty relationship with them, there is no evidence that they were believed to have done so on any given occasion. The gods were the guarantors of the royal treaties and of the oaths of allegiance, but they were not parties to them.[112] When a people is searching for the explanation of some disaster inflicted on them by the gods, they are quite likely to feel guilty of breaking the treaty, not with the gods, but with their human overlords. Thus the Arabs, after a series of unsuccessful rebellions against Assyria, asked themselves:

> 'Why have such calamities befallen the land of Arabia?' (and they answered themselves) 'It is because we have not observed the great covenants with Aššur, and have sinned against the kindness of Aššurbanipal, the king whom Enlil loves' (Annals of Aššurbanipal, col. ix, ll. 70-74; Streck, *Assurbanipal*, II, pp. 78-79;[113] *ANET*, p. 300).

The Babylonian and Assyrian laws are decrees of the king: Marduk (according to the prologue) or Šamaš (according to the relief on the stele and the epilogue) merely commissioned Hammurabi 'to guide the people aright'.[114] The Akkadian prayers frequently complain that what the gods require is *not* known.[115]

In contrast, Israelite prayers are set firmly in the context of Yahweh's covenant with Israel, Solomon's list of occasions for prayer (1 Kgs 8.22-53) envisages possible future breakdowns in Israel's relationship with God, whose covenant is deposited in the ark in the temple being dedicated (v. 21) and who has a reputation for keeping the covenant with his servants and acting loyally towards them (v. 23). The prayers themselves refer explicitly to the covenant. In one of national psalms the people say:

---

110. Laessøe, *People*, pp. 147-48, 153.
111. Widengren, *Psalms of Lamentation*, p. 289.
112. R. de Vaux, *Ancient Israel: Its Life and Institutions* (trans. J. McHugh; London: Darton, Longman & Todd, 1961), p. 148; McCarthy, *Treaty and Covenant*, pp. 92-94; Saggs, *Greatness*, p. 429.
113. M. Streck, *Assurbanipal und die letzten assyrischen Königs bis zum Untergange Nineveh's* (VAB, 7; Leipzig: J.C. Hinrichs, 1916).
114. *ANET*, p. 165.
115. Widengren, *Psalms of Lamentation*, pp. 99-100.

> We have not forgotten you,
> We have not betrayed your covenant,
> Our heart has not defected,
> Our steps have not left your way (Ps. 44.18-19 [EVV 17-18]).

Similarly, Jeremiah appeals to God to remember his promise:

> Remember, do not break you covenant with us (Jer. 14.21).

There are several other examples.[116] And when psalmists speak of walking in Yahweh's paths (Ps. 17.5) or refer to specific evil deeds avoided (Ps. 7.5 [EVV 4]), they have Yahweh's known law in mind.

We have already remarked that the analogy between the letters and the prayers is chiefly one of content. The following chapters (3–8) will offer detailed evidence in support of this view. Each of the leading themes common to both types of material will be analysed in turn.

---

116. Pss. 25.10, 14; 74.20; 89.40 (EVV 39).

3

PROTESTATIONS OF LOYALTY AND CONFESSION OF FAULTS

Protestations of Innocence or Loyalty

In a number of biblical psalms and prayers the person praying makes a point of declaring his innocence. In Ps. 26.1-8, for example, the psalmist claims that his life will survive the most searching test of his loyalty to Yahweh:

> Judge me, Yahweh, for I have lived blamelessly,
> I have trusted in Yahweh without faltering.
> Examine me, Yahweh, and test me,
> Try my character and my heart.
> For the thought of your loyalty I keep before me,
> I have lived trusting in your faithfulness.
> I have not associated with worthless people,
> Nor do I join the company of schemers;
> I hate the gathering of evildoers,
> And do not sit down with the wicked.
> I will wash my hands in proof of innocence,
> And I will go round your altar, Yahweh,
> To make the sound of thanksgiving heard,
> And to relate all your wonderful deeds.
> Yahweh, I love your dwelling, your house,[1]
> The place where your glory abides.

Similarly, in Ps. 17.1-5 the psalmist is certain that God has no fault to find with him: although the text of the passage is uncertain, the general sense is clear. Ps. 7.4-6 (EVV 3-5) has the form of a conditional curse upon oneself.[2]

> Yahweh, my God, if I have done this,
> If my hands are stained with injustice,
> If I have done a bad turn to a friend,

---

1. Or, with LXX, 'I love the beauty of your house'.
2. See Job 31.7-8; Ps. 137.5-6; also 1 Sam. 3.17; 14.44; 25.22 LXX; 1 Kgs 2.23; 19.2; 20.10; 2 Kgs 6.31; Ruth 1.17; J. Pedersen, *Der Eid bei den Semiten* (Studien zur Geschichte und Kultur des Islamischen Orients; Strasbourg: Trübner, 1914), pp. 113-14; Gunkel and Begrich, *Einleitung*, §6.26.

Or let one who harassed me without cause go free,
Then may the enemy pursue me and overtake me,
Grind my life into the ground,
And lay my honour in the dust.

Hans Schmidt[3] interpreted these and other psalms in which the innocence of the psalmist is either expressed or presupposed as 'prayers of the accused', that is, as forms for the 'oath of purgation' to be sworn in the situation described in 1 Kgs 8.31-32:[4]

When a man sins against his neighbour and is required to swear an oath, and he comes and swears it before your altar in this house, hear it in heaven and act: judge your servants, condemning the wicked, bringing the consequences of his way upon him, but acquitting the innocent, giving him what his innocence deserves.

There are, however, several considerations which make this unlikely. It may be granted that these psalms are couched in the language of the courts, and the passage quoted from Psalm 7 may well be modelled on a formal oath. But the declarations of innocence are too comprehensive and general to be the reply to specific charges,[5] and the dangers to which the psalmist is exposed are not those attendant on wrongful conviction, but, as in other psalms, those which the malice of enemies may devise (see, e.g., Pss. 7.2-3 [EVV 1-2]; 17.7-12). Other passages which set out a form of words for a situation like this (Num. 5.11-28; Deut. 21.1-9) suggest that the reference to the allegation would be quite specific.[6] Even more important, perhaps, is the fact that prayers that include this motif are found outside the psalter also, assigned to situations where accusation of crimes or sins is not in question. When Hezekiah prays

Yahweh, remember that I have been faithful and devoted to you, and have done what is good in your eyes (2 Kgs 20.3 = Isa. 38.3),

it is not because he has been accused of any crime. Similarly, when Jeremiah pleads that he has not been given to merrymaking (Jer. 15.17) and that he has not deserted his post (Jer. 17.16), it is in the context of his own complaint

---

3. Schmidt, *Das Gebet der Angeklagten; idem*, 'Die Gebete der Angeklagten, im Alten Testament', in D.C.Simpson (ed.), *Old Testament Essays: Papers Read before the Society for Old Testament Study at its Eighteenth Meeting at Keble College Oxford September 27th to 30th, 1927* (London: Charles Griffin, 1927), pp. 143-55; *idem, Die Psalmen* (HAT, 15; Tübingen: J.C.B. Mohr [Paul Siebeck], 1934), on the psalms in question.

4. Cf. Exod. 22.9-10 (EVV 10-11); Deut. 21.1-9; Num. 5.19-22; CH, §§20; 103; 106; 107; 126; 131; Laws of Ešnunna, §37.

5. Cf. H. Ringgren, *The Faith of the Psalmists* (London: SCM Press, 1963), pp. 71-72.

6. Cf. J.H. Eaton, *The Psalms* (Torch Commentaries; London: SCM Press, 1967), pp. 85-86.

about his sufferings as a prophet. The same motif can occur in one of the so-called communal laments (Ps. 44.18-23 [EVV 17-22]); again a trial background is out of the question. Protestations of innocence are felt to be appropriate in more contexts than that of accusation in a formal trial. The innocence of the suppliants is advanced either as a reason why God should help them,[7] or as a ground of confidence that he will.[8] It is taken for granted that the prayer of the wicked will not be heard:

> Yahweh is far from the wicked,
> But he hears the prayer of the good (Prov. 15.29);

> If I countenance wickedness in my heart
> The Lord will not listen (Ps. 66.18).

This conclusion is confirmed when the same feature is found in certain Akkadian psalms, and the context is clearly that of sickness, which the suppliant feels to be undeserved. In a hymn and lament addressed to Ištar, Aššur-nasirpal I claims to have feared the goddess, provided her sacrifices and restored images and temples.[9] Aššurbanipal says: 'I have done good to God and men, to dead and living'.[10] Both say they are being treated 'like one who does not reverence (the god's) divinity'.[11] In Sumerian letter prayers the protestation of innocence appears along with the recalling of one's past service and present rank as something which recommends the suppliant for future favours from the deity.[12] Ramesses II pleaded his innocence of any transgression or neglect of Amun's commands:

> I have not transgressed a plan that you have decreed!...
> Have I not built for you a great many monuments?
> Have I not filled your temple with my captives?...
> I have given to you all my possessions by testament,
> I have dedicated all lands together to you in order to endow your offerings.
> I have caused tens of thousands of cattle to be presented to you,
> and all aromatic herbs.
> I have not left out (any) good deed, so as not to do them in your court
> (Poem on the Battle of Qadeš, ll. 96, 98-99, 101-104;
> Davies, *Inscriptions*, pp, 62-65).

---

7.   Heiler, *Prayer*, p. 256; Castellino, *Lamentazioni*, p. 7.

8.   Castellino, *Lamentazioni*, p. 7; Barucq, *L'expression*, p. 348.

9.   *SAHG* B 14, ll. 16-21, 31-40 (*HPD*, pp. 498-500; *Before the Muses*, III.4[a], pp. 241-42).

10.   *SAHG* B 17, l. 1. See also Widengren, *Psalms of Lamentation*, p. 140.

11.   *SAHG* B 14, l. R4 (*HPD*, p. 500); *SAHG* B 17, l. 12. Cf. *SAHG* B 61, l. 68 (*HPD*, p. 192; *Before the Muses*, III.27[b], p. 508). Widengren, *Psalms of Lamentation*, pp. 179-81; *Ludlul bel nemeqi* II, ll. 12-22; *ANET*, pp. 434-35; *CoS*, I.153, p. 488; W.G. Lambert, *Babylonian Wisdom Literature* (Oxford: Clarendon Press, 1960), pp. 10-11, 22, 38-39.

12.   Hallo, 'Individual Prayer', p. 79.

Detailed declarations of innocence also occur in Egyptian funerary texts, and thus contribute to the 'ideal biography' of the deceased.[13] If these prayers are to be regarded as in any sense the reply to an accusation, it is an accusation believed to be *implied* in the gods' treatment of the persons concerned, not a formal accusation of a specific crime in court.

It was natural that such protestation should have a prominent place in prayer, because it has an equally prominent place in the analogous secular situation. The letters illustrate this clearly. Correspondents, who are generally provincial governors or royal officials of some kind, are often at pains to remind the king of their loyalty. Rib-Hadda's appeal to his record of loyalty to the previous pharaoh has already been quoted. But perhaps the most vehement protests in the Amarna letters come from those whose loyalty was rightly suspect. Rib-Hadda, who probably did rule and defend Byblos in the pharaoh's interests, was threatened through a great part of his career by 'Abdi-aširta of Amurru and his son and successor Aziru. Now Aziru not only harassed his fellow vassals in Syria: he also made a treaty of alliance with the Hittite king Šuppiluliumaš.[14] Nevertheless he can protest complete loyalty:

> Now may the king, my lord, know that I am your servant for ever. I do not deviate from the orders of my lord. My lord, from the very first I have wanted to enter the service of the king, my lord, but the magnates of Sumur do not permit me. Now, of dereliction of duty or the slightest thing against the king I am innocent. The king, my lord, knows who the real rebels are. And whatever the request of the king, my lord, I will grant it (EA 157, ll. 6-19).

Similarly, Lab'ayu (of Shechem?)[15] is complained of in the letters of Šuwardata of Hebron (EA 280), 'Abdi-Heba of Jerusalem (EA 289) and Biridiya of Megiddo (EA 244; 245), and is probably to be identified with the 'Apiru chief mentioned in EA 366, but he nevertheless protests his loyalty:

> The fact is that I am a loyal servant of the king! I am not a rebel and I am not delinquent in duty. I have not held back my payments of tribute; I have not held back anything requested by my commissioner (EA 254, ll. 10-15; *ANET*, p. 486; Oppenheim, *Letters*, No. 68).[16]

    13. *ANET*, pp. 34-36; Barucq, *L'expression*, pp. 368, 380; Dalglish, *Psalm Fifty-One*, pp. 15-16; Westermann, *Praise and Lament*, pp. 43-44.

    14. E.F. Weidner, *Politische Documente aus Kleinasien: Die Staatsverträge in akkadischer Sprache aus dem Archiv aus Boghazköi* (Boghazköi-Studien, 8-9; Leipzig: J.C. Hinrichs, 1923), no. 5, pp. 70-75.

    15. See E.F. Campbell, 'The Amarna Letters and the Amarna Period', *BA* 23 (1960), pp. 2-22 (19); reprinted in Campbell and Freedman (eds.), *The Biblical Archaeologist Reader 3*, pp. 54-75 (72).

    16. Cf. R.S. Hess, 'Smitten Ant Bites Back: Rhetorical Forms in the Amarna Correspondence from Shechem', in J.C. de Moor and W.G.E. Watson (eds.), *Verse in Ancient Near Eastern Prose* (AOAT, 42; Kevelaer: Butzon & Bercker; Neukirchen–Vluyn: Neukirchener Verlag, 1993), pp. 95-111.

This may have been only a show of loyalty for political reasons,[17] but it is interesting that even these men should feel the need to clear themselves in the pharaoh's eyes.

Assyrian vassals and officials protest their loyalty in similar terms. Merodach-baladan, who was later to rebel against Assyria in the time of Sargon II and Sennacherib, earlier assisted Tiglath-pileser III to put down the rebellion of Mukin-zeri.[18] He expressed his loyalty to the Assyrian king in terms that were routinely reproduced by Babylonian officials of the period:

> I would go as substitute (in death) for my lord (ND 2389, l. 2; *Nimrud Letters*, pp. 10, 17-18).[19]

A Nimrud letter, possibly on a question of land tenure, contains this vehement passage:

> Indeed it is true. The king will certainly not believe me. I am a dog. The king my lord has wrought truth for the gods; would I send an untruthful message to the king my lord? (ND 2380 + 2396, ll. R4-11; *Nimrud Letters*, pp. 104-106).

A Babylonian official rebuts an accusation that he has failed to reply to a communication from the king:

> I do indeed send my communications to the king my lord. Someone has not allowed the royal messenger to get through quickly to the king or has sent him away. As soon as the communication of the king came before me, I had an answer despatched to the king, as I wrote it. If the messenger does not pass it on, the king should not set it to the fault of (me) his servant (ND 2478, ll. 13-24; *Nimrud Letters*, pp. 11, 53-55).

An official in Syria, accused of failing to provide food and animal fodder for the capital, details what he has done and lays the blame on those who are responsible for other stages on the journey:

> Now the king my lord certainly knows, that they are rebellious (while) we [are obedient] (ND 2495, ll. 34-36; *Nimrud Letters*, pp. 173-75; SAA 1, No. 172).

A letter from Marduk-šumu-usur, the chief diviner of Esarhaddon and Aššur-banipal, complains of being robbed by the provincial governor of a grainfield

---

17. K.A. Kitchen, *Suppiluliuma and the Amarna Pharaohs* (Liverpool Monographs in Archaeology and Oriental Studies; Liverpool: Liverpool University Press, 1962), p. 14; E.F. Campbell, *The Chronology of the Amarna Letters* (Baltimore: The Johns Hopkins University Press, 1964), p. 66.

18. For Merodach-baladan (Marduk-apla-iddina) and Mukin-zeri see *Prosopography*, 2/II L-N, *s.v.* Marduk-apla-iddina §1, and Mukin-zeri §1.

19. Cf. ND 2695, ll. 1-3; ND 2689, ll. 2-3; ND 2065, ll. 2-3; ND 2478, l. 2; ND 2710, l. 2; ND 2388, ll. 1-2; ND 2398, ll. 1-2; ND 2681, ll. 1-2; ND 2403, ll. R 3-4; ND 2412, ll. 2-3; ND 2661, l. 2; ND 2667, ll. 2-3 (*Nimrud Letters*, pp. 18-19, 51-56, 57-59, 63-64, 74-75, 79, 89-92).

given to him by the king's father. He mentions his loyalty as a reason why the king should intervene:

> The king, my lord, knows that I am a poor man, keep the watch of the king, my lord, (and) am guilty of no negligence within the palace (ABL 421 [*LAS*, No. 114; SAA 10, No. 173], ll. 17-R4; Laessøe, *People*, p. 97).

Nabû-hamatua rebuts the charge of negligence:

> The king, my lord, should not say: 'He is a negligent servant; he does not do his work'. I drive the servants of the king, my lord, day and night (ABL 1068 [SAA 5, No. 211], ll. R2-8).

Na'id-Marduk, governor of the Sealand in the reign of Esarhaddon, in a letter to Zakutu, the queen mother, couples a request for troops with an expression of loyalty:

> My lord should know that my heart is completely devoted to my lord's house (ABL 917, [SAA 18, No. 85] ll. R14-15).

Another letter is thought to be from the Sealanders to Esarhaddon confirming the truth of what the governor claims:

> When we heard that the king was angry with our lord, we became afraid, saying: 'Our lord has committed no sin in the king's eyes', inasmuch as he prays every morning and evening to Šamaš and Bel for the life of the king, his lord; his heart is completely devoted to the king, his lord, he is despised because of the king, his lord, and his house has been destroyed because he grasps the feet of the king his lord (ABL 958 [SAA 18, No. 88], ll. R3-10).

Mannu-ki-Libbali declares that he is not implicated in a certain matter in terms very similar to the oath of purgation:

> I swear that I did not know (and) did not learn about this matter, that I am not implicated in it... If I am implicated in this matter, let the king, my lord, punish me (ABL 211 [SAA 16, No. 78], ll. 6-9, 15-17).

The integrity of these men and others who protest their loyalty[20] may still be open to question in some instances,[21] but it is significant that the professions themselves should be expected to weigh with the king.

The occasions for these protestations vary. It is well known that both in the Amarna letters[22] and in the Assyrian letters[23] vassals and officials accused

---

20. ABL 317 (SAA 5, No. 243), ll. 8-11; 360 (*LAS*, No. 156; SAA 10, No. 215), ll. 6-9; 556, ll. R7-8.

21. Waterman, *Royal Correspondence*, IV, p. 23.

22. Albright, 'Amarna Letters', p. 104; Kitchen, *Suppiluliuma*, p. 14; Campbell, *Chronology*, p. 66.

23. Waterman, *Royal Correspondence*, IV, p. 23.

each other of disloyalty to the crown, and sometimes these accusations are repeated in the kings' letters to the men under suspicion. For example, there are complaints about Aziru in the letters of Akizzi of Qatna (EA 55, ll. 44-47) and Abi-Milku of Tyre (EA 151, ll. 59-68). The latter mentions an alliance Aziru has made with the ruler of Qadeš, and this accusation is taken up by the pharaoh in a letter to Aziru:

> Now the king has heard as follows. 'You are at peace with the ruler of Qidša. The two of you take food and strong drink together'. And it is true. Why do you act so? Why are you at peace with a ruler with whom the king is fighting?... What happened to you among them that you are not on the side of the king, your lord? (EA 162, ll. 22-25, 28-29)

No reply of Aziru to this particular charge has been preserved, but clearly his professions of loyalty must be related to the accusations which have been made against him.

Sometimes the correspondent quotes the slander and rebuts it. Yamsûm protests his loyalty in a series of letters to Zimri-lim prompted by the accusations Hâya-sûmû has made against him:

> My lord gave me instructions in these terms: 'You are to go to the town of Ilân-surâ, and there you are to watch over what I will command you'. According to the instructions of my lord, I have conscientiously fulfilled my role and I have not made any mistakes nor left anything undone with respect to my lord's business. If I have not confirmed what I have heard here and there and my eyes have seen, I have not written about it to my lord. It is possible that once or twice I have not confirmed a report, but in no case have I lied, for I could not lie to my lord. Now someone has sought out my lord and slandered me in these terms: 'Yasîm-El has entrusted to Yamsûm Numaean slaves. He has disregarded the oath taken by Itûr-Mêr and my lord'. I swear that I have not seen anything in the hands of Yasîm-El or in the hands of soldiers, that I have not brought anything into the town of Ilân-surâ and that I have not hidden the matter from my lord: if not, who will rescue me one day or the other from the hands of my lord? (ARM XXVI.302, ll. 4-27 [*AEM*, I/2, p. 56]).[24]

Similarly, the letters in which Bel-ibni, a Babylonian official in the reigns of Sargon II and Sennacherib,[25] protests his innocence of the things he has been accused of must be seen against the background of specific charges (ABL 283; 793; Oppenheim, *Letters*, No. 90). But in other instances the protestation of loyalty is introduced simply as a reason why the king should act on the subject's behalf: he deserves it. This is true of the occurrences of the motif in the letters of Rib-Hadda and Marduk-šumu-usur which have been cited. It is clear therefore that the motif is not confined to situations in which

24. Cf. ARM XXVI.326, ll. 26-36 (*AEM*, I/2, p. 95).

25. To be distinguished from Bel-ibni, governor of the Sealand in the reign of Aššur-banipal. See *Prosopography*, 1/II, *s.v.* Bel-ibni, §8.

the correspondent is required to clear himself of formal charges. Even where an oath of purgation occurs, as in a letter from Zeru-ibni to Sargon, it is an informal stylistic variation, not part of a judicial process:

> As to Marduk-eriba about whom the king, my lord, wrote to me, if I have put Marduk-eriba in irons, let them release his shackles and put them on my own feet! If not, let them pull the tongue out of the throat of the man who lied to the king, my lord! (ABL 154 [SAA 1, No. 205], ll. 4-11).

The prominence of this feature in the letters, and its general character as a ground of appeal, make it likely that its occurrence in the biblical prayers is equally general in character. The evidence from the letters thus confirms the view that Schmidt's thesis should be rejected.

Confession of Faults

Declarations of innocence and faithfulness are not, of course, always appropriate. In Old Testament prayers, the worshippers are often only too well aware that they have sinned, and so they confess it.[26] The confession of sin becomes a dominant feature of post-exilic prayers, partly because the Deuteronomistic theology would not allow that disaster could be due to any lack of faithfulness on God's side, and partly because Jewish national hopes continued to be disappointed.[27]

The motif is also found in non-biblical prayers. Penitence is rare in Egyptian literature, though there are some late instances.[28] The early Sumerian prayers also lack explicit confession of sin,[29] but it is prominent in certain Akkadian psalms, particularly of the *eršahunga* type.[30] The self-confessed motive of these confessions is the appeasing of the gods, as an important inscription of Aššurbanipal makes clear:

> Their angry gods and wrathful goddesses I appeased with intercessory rites and laments to quieten the heart (*ARAB*, II, §797).[31]

26. Pss. 25.11; 38.19 (EVV 18); 51; 69.6 (EVV 5); 79.9; Exod. 32.31-32; Judg.10.10, 15; 1 Sam. 12.10; 2 Sam. 24.10, 17; Jer. 14.7, 20; Lam. 3.42; Ezra 9.6; Dan. 9.5; Tob. 3.3; Bar. 2.12; *Prayer of Azariah* 6-7; cf. Heiler, *Prayer*, pp. 258-59.

27. P.A.H. de Boer, *De Voorbede in het Oude Testament* (Leiden: E.J. Brill, 1943 = *OTS* 3), p. 151; Westermann, 'Struktur', pp. 71-72 = *Forschung*, pp. 296-97; *Praise and Lament*, p. 202.

28. Barucq, *L'expression*, pp. 30, 369-70, 504; Dalglish, *Psalm Fifty-One*, p. 8; Blackman, 'Egyptian Research', p. 196; BM 589 Hymn to Ptah; Turin 102 (*ANET*, p. 381).

29. *SAHG*, pp. 36; Hallo, 'Individual Prayer', p. 82.

30. Dalglish, *Psalm Fifty-One*, p. 22 n. 21, lists twenty-six examples. Cf. *HPD*, pp. 139-68. The *eršahunga* is a prayer 'to calm the heart' of a divinity.

31. Quoted by Dalglish, *Psalm Fifty-One*, p. 33 n. 64.

Confession of guilt is not frequent in the letters: possibly correspondents thought that guilt could be hidden longer from the king than from the god, or that the mercy of the god was more certain than that of the king. Excuses are relatively frequent.[32] But the occasional confession does occur. Even the truculent Lab'ayu admits to having entered Gezer, the city of Milk-ilu, though he seeks to show his action in a favourable light (EA 253, ll. 18-22; EA 254, ll. 20-29; Oppenheim, *Letters*, No. 68).[33] The writer of a letter to Esarhaddon (possibly Adad-šumu-usur)[34] confesses to an offence, but there is no indication what it was:

> I committed a serious crime against the house of my lords. I (deserved) to be killed, not to be kept alive. Yet the king, my lord, had mercy on his dog (ABL 620 [SAA 16, No. 36], ll. 3-5).

The Old Testament itself contains two or three instances of subjects confessing to the king that they have sinned against him (1 Sam. 25.28; 2 Sam. 19.19-20; 2 Kgs 18.14). These instances, biblical and non-biblical, are a sufficient reminder that the confession of sin is not a purely religious phenomenon, but has its secular analogue.

'What is my Sin?'

Midway between the protestation of innocence and the confession of sin comes the hesitant query: What is my sin? This arises in a situation where the suppliant cannot explain a present calamity as the consequence of any known sin, but is prepared to admit that he may have sinned unwittingly through ignorance. Thus the psalmist says:

> Who can understand his accidental mistakes?
> Hold me innocent of secret faults (Ps. 19.13 [EVV 12]).

Job asks to know how he has offended:

> I will say to God, do not condemn me,
> Tell me what charge your are bringing against me (Job 10.2);
>
> How many evils and sins have I committed?
> Tell me my transgression and my sin (Job 13.23).

---

32. ABL 202; 276 (SAA 10, No. 371) (cf. Olmstead, *History of Assyria*, pp. 356, 402); for excuses in Egyptian prayers, see Barucq, *L'expression*, p. 385.

33. See E.F. Campbell, in G.E. Wright, *Shechem: Biography of a Biblical City* (London: Gerald Duckworth, 1965), pp. 197-98.

34. K. Deller, 'Die Briefe des Adad-šumu-usur', in Röllig (ed.), Lišan mithurti, pp. 45-64 (58), assigned this letter to Adad-šumu-usur, but S. Parpola, *LAS*, II, p. 107, disputed the attribution on the ground of certain spellings.

The same anxious uncertainty haunts the non-biblical prayers. In the Sumerian letter prayers, to say 'I do not know my guilt' or 'I do not know my sin, of my sin I have no knowledge' is little more than a variation on the protestation of innocence,[35] but in the Akkadian psalms the suppliant genuinely wants to know how he has gone wrong. He confesses sins known and unknown.[36] He asks: Who can understand the ways of God?[37] He wants to know how he has neglected the goddess,[38] what he has done.[39] The speaker in a well known late Sumerian psalm knows neither which god or goddess he has offended nor what his offence is:

> O god whom I know or do not know, my transgressions are many; great are my sins;
> O goddess whom I know or do not know, my transgressions are many; great are my sins.
> The transgression that I have committed, indeed I do not know;
> The sin that I have done, indeed I do not know.
> The forbidden thing that I have eaten, indeed I do not know;
> The prohibited place on which I have set foot, indeed I do not know
>   (*SAHG* 45, ll. 24-29 [p. 226]; *HPD*, p. 141; *ANET*, p. 391).

The most remarkable product of this feeling of uncertainty is the (second) plague prayer of the Hittite king Muršiliš II (*CTH* 378; *ANET*, pp. 394-96; *CoS*, I.60 [Second Prayer]). The king has been unable to recall any obvious sin for which the plague might have been sent. He has prayed to all the gods and asked them to establish the reason for the plague:

> Either let it be established by an omen, or let me see it in a dream, or let a prophet declare it (§2).[40]

But these entreaties have had no effect so far on the course of the plague. Now two tablets have come to light which suggest that certain sins of his father may be responsible (§§3-5). For the sake of his people the king shoulders his father's guilt and confesses it:

> It is only too true that man is sinful. My father sinned and transgressed against the word of the Hattian storm-god, my lord. But I have not sinned in any respect. It is only too true, however, that the father's sin falls upon the son. So, my father's sin has fallen on me (§9).

---

35. Hallo, 'Individual Prayer', p. 79.
36. *SAHG* B 19, l. 19 (*HPD*, p. 208; *Before the Muses*, III.49[d], pp. 630-31); B 43, l. 18 (*HPD*, p. 170; *Before the Muses*, III.44[a], p. 586); B 44, l. 9 (*HPD*, p. 341).
37. *SAHG* B 43, l. 11 (*HPD*, p. 170; *Before the Muses*, III.44[a], p. 585).
38. *SAHG* B 14, l. 41 (*HPD*, p. 500; *Before the Muses*, III.4[a], p. 242).
39. *SAHG* B 61, l. 67 (*HPD*, p. 192; *Before the Muses*, III.27[b], p. 508).
40. Cf. the prayer of Kantuzilis, *CTH* 373; *ANET*, p. 400.

The reason for confessing the sin of one's forebears[41] is here clearly seen to be lack of awareness of any serious sins of one's own, just as confession of the sins of one's youth[42] and former iniquities[43] indicate that the worshipper is not conscious of present or recent sins. Elsewhere, where it accompanies the confession of one's own sin, it is included so as to cover all possible grounds for the god's displeasure.[44]

The same uncertainty about one's offence is found in the letters. Many of them ask what the offence is that has been committed. A subject or vassal of the Hittite king Tudhaliyas IV (1265–1230 BCE), suspected of transferring his allegiance to the Assyrian king Shalmaneser I, asks what it is he is supposed to have done:

> In what respect have I now offended against my father? (*CTH* 179; *HDT*, No. 25, §4, p. 151).[45]

The Assyrian letters provide a number of examples.[46] Bel-ibni reports to Aššurbanipal a query of this kind on behalf of the Elamites:

> Send these words by a courier to the palace, 'Now Elam has sent its messenger to the king of Assyria, with this message: "What is the sin which we have committed against you?" In regard to all this you are being negligent' (ABL 792, ll. 8-12).

Here is a very vigorous protest, probably from the time of Sargon:

> Concerning what the kind, my lord, w[rote to me], 'I gave you [explicit orde]rs regarding the work on […], but you do not obey me'—if I did not obey the king, my lord, whom else would I obey? Now the king, my lord, has (already) three or four times written to me in this manner; how can I live? My heart does not beat, my blood has dried up in my veins (ABL 455 [SAA 15, No. 30], ll. 4-14).

A letter from Aššurbanipal to Nabû-ušabši, governor of Uruk, contains the king's reply to such a query:

---

41. Cf. Widengren, *Psalms of Lamentation*, pp. 170-71. Seux, *HPD*, p. 171 n. 22, believes that the sins confessed at *SAHG* B 43, ll. 22-23 (*Before the Muses*, III.44[a], l. 21, p. 586) may be sins committed *against* family members rather than *by* them.

42. Ps. 25.7; *SAHG* B 43, l. 18 (*HPD*, p. 170; *Before the Muses*, III.44[a], p. 586); Widengren, *Psalms of Lamentation*, pp. 98-99.

43. Ps. 79.8.

44. Ps. 51.7 (EVV 5); *SAHG* B 43, ll. 16-24 (*HPD*, pp. 170-71; *Before the Muses*, III.44[a], p. 586); Widengren, *Psalms of Lamentation*, pp. 97-98.

45. H. Klengel, 'Zum Brief eines Königs von Hanigalbat (IBoT I 34)', *Orientalia* NS 32 (1963), pp. 280-91.

46. In addition to the letters quoted below, see ND 2673, ll. R12-13 (*Nimrud Letters*, pp. 136-39); ABL 390, ll. 6-8; 530, ll. R2-13; 885 (SAA 16, No. 34), ll. R16-17.

Now [why] have you spoken, saying, 'What is my crime?' It is not your crime,
It is the crime of your subordinates, the governors, to whom I wrote (but) they
do not come, are not staying with you, and they are not doing the work...
(ABL 543, ll. 9-15).

Promise of Future Loyalty

A further variation on this theme is the promise of future loyalty. In the biblical psalms this is at it s simplest a vow to offer sacrifice (Pss. 54.8 [EVV 6];
66.14-16 [EVV 13-15]; cf. Gen. 28.20-22; Judg. 11.30-31), or the praise
which Yahweh prefers to sacrifice (Ps. 51.17-18 [EVV 15-16]; 69.31-32 [EVV
30-31]). Similar promises are made in non-biblical prayers. In a Sumerian
letter prayer the suppliant says that he will 'dwell in your gates and sing your
praises...and proclaim your exaltation'.[47] Akkadian psalms frequently close
with a promise to sing the praise of the god or goddess when the prayer is
answered.[48] Sometimes, however, the biblical psalmist promises loyalty of a
more comprehensive kind. Thus in Psalm 101 the suppliant (probably the
king at his enthronement[49]) says:

> I will keep prudently to a blameless way:
> When will you come to me?
> I will behave irreproachably
> Within my house,
> I will not set before my eyes
> Any wicked thing.
> I hate any crooked dealing,
> It shall not involve me.
> I will put away corrupt motives from me:
> I will not tolerate a wicked person.
> Him who slanders his neighbour in secret
> I will get rid of,
> Him who has a proud look and an arrogant spirit
> I will not endure.
> My eyes will be upon the loyal in the land:
> They shall be in my household.
> He who conducts himself blamelessly
> Shall serve me.
> The man who practises deceit
> Shall not remain in my house,

---

47. Hallo, 'Individual Prayer', p. 79.
48. *SAHG* B 14, ll. R 26-27 (*HPD*, p. 501); B 41, ll. 27-28 (*HPD*, p. 275); B 44, l. 17
(*HPD*, p. 340); B 45, l. 21 (*HPD*, p. 131); B 46, ll. 79-80 (*HPD*, p. 449; *Before the Muses*,
III.44[b], ll. 76-79, p. 592); B 47, l. 78 (*HPD*, p. 453); B 50, l. 25 (*HPD*, p. 314); B 51, l.
31 (*HPD*, p. 316). Cf. Hallo, 'Individual Prayer', p. 81.
49. Mowinckel, *Psalms*, I, pp. 67-68.

He who tells lies
Shall not keep his place before me.
Day by day I will root out
All the wrongdoers of the land,
And so cut off from Yahweh's city
All who practise evil (Ps. 101.2-8).[50]

The clearest parallels to a promise of loyalty of this order are to be found in the letters rather than in the non-biblical psalms. In a letter from Nimrud, Nabû-etir reports that the governor of a certain district had promised tribute as a result of punitive action:

I myself sent a message for the king my lord to the governor. In this manner he replied to me, saying: 'The people will cultivate as much as is at their disposal. I will not hold one back. I will send everyone out and will deliver to the king my lord' (ND 2649, ll. 11-23; *Nimrud Letters*, pp. 206-207).

Bel-ibni writes as follows to Aššurbanipal upon his appointment as governor of the Sealand:

Now the king my lord [sees] the faithfulness of his servant with the house of his lord, how indeed (it is), when I keep the watch of the king my lord—a servant, a friend, and a sharp blade am I [in] the hand of the king my lord (ABL 521, ll. 18-22).[51]

The foregoing has shown that pleas in the biblical psalms based on worshippers' conduct, whether they declare themselves innocent or penitent or mystified, have close parallels in the letters which passed between subjects and their kings, as well as in non-biblical prayers. Since there is no reason to believe that there was any literary dependence of the biblical prayers on the non-biblical, the presence of these pleas in the psalms is most simply explained as due to the recognition of the analogy between the secular and religious situations.

50. It is not certain that the imperfect tenses in this psalm should be translated as futures: if they are taken as past or present tenses, then the passage quoted becomes a protestation of loyalty rather than a promise.

51. Cf. ABL 283, ll. R17-20; EA 64, ll. 14-17; 232, ll. 12-20; ND 2798, l. R6; ND 2683, l. 36 (*Nimrud Letters*, pp. 147-48, 290-92).

4

DESCRIPTION OF PLIGHT

The second feature of the biblical prayers that is paralleled in many letters is the suppliant's description of his plight.[1] This is nearly always a life-threatening situation:[2]

> Have mercy upon me, Yahweh, for I am in trouble:
> My eyes, my throat, my belly, are wasting away with frustration.
> For my life is ending in grief,
> And my years in groaning,
> My strength is failing because of my distress[3]
> And my bones are wasting away.
> I am held in scorn by all my enemies
> And my neighbours shake their heads.[4]
> My acquaintances are afraid of me,
> Those who see me out of doors run away from me.
> I am forgotten, one of mind like one who is dead:
> I am like a broken pot.
> For I hear many whispering,
> There is terror on every side,
> While they gang up against me,
> And plot to take my life (Ps. 31.10-14 [EVV 9-13]).[5]

This psalmist complains both of sickness[6] and of the intrigues of his enemies,[7] and these are the principal themes of all the individual laments. In royal psalms and communal laments the distress described is that caused by defeat in battle, most notably the fall of Jerusalem to the Babylonians.[8] The

---

1. Gunkel and Begrich, *Einleitung*, §§4.10; 6.11, 17. This may take the form of a narrative or a portrayal, or a blend of both (§6.11 [p. 216; ET p. 155]).
2. Gunkel and Begrich, *Einleitung*, §6.5.
3. Reading בְּעֶנְי with Symmachus instead of בַּעֲוֹנִי.
4. Reading מָנוֹד instead of מְאֹד.
5. Cf. Pss. 22.13-22 (EVV 12-21); 55; 69; 102.4-12 (EVV 3-11).
6. Gunkel and Begrich, *Einleitung*, §6.6.
7. Gunkel and Begrich, *Einleitung*, §6.8.
8. Pss. 44.10-17 (EVV 9-16); 60.3-5 (EVV 1-3); 74; 79; 80.6-7, 13-14, 16-17 (EVV 5-6, 12-13, 15-16); 89.39-46 (EVV 38-45); Isa. 63.18; 64.11; Jer. 10.25; Lamentations (*passim*).

persecution by Antiochus Epiphanes also draws out descriptions of the plight of the Jews.[9]

The complaints in non-Israelite prayers are similar in content.[10] In Akkadian prayers sickness is the dominant theme.[11] Discord, strife and rebellion aggravate the distress caused by sickness, especially when the sufferer is a king. We may instance the well-known lament of Aššurbanipal:

> Why have sickness, sorrow, (wasting) and ruin come upon me?
> Discord in the country and fierce quarrelling in my household never leave me;
> Insurrection and slander are continually plotted against me.
> Deep affliction and bodily pain have bowed down my figure;
> I spend the day groaning and complaining (*SAHG* B 17, ll. 2-6).

What is the purpose of these descriptions or narrations of distress? In the case of the Akkadian prayers, the answer to this question is complicated by the presence of magical ideas. Although magic is not always presupposed as the cause of the distress, and even some of the *šu-illa* prayers, which were those most closely associated with magical rituals, lack any reference to magic,[12] nevertheless it is very common for sickness to be regarded as the work of magicians and demons.[13] Thus it is likely that one reason for cataloguing the sufferings in detail is that this is required for a successful exorcism: the affliction must be named before it can be removed.[14] But the suppliant has at least been allowed to fall into the hands of evil powers by the god,[15] and so

9. Dan. 9.16-19; 1 Macc. 3.45, 51.

10. For Egyptian prayers, see Barucq, *L'expression*, pp. 386-87; for Sumerian letter prayers, see Hallo, 'Individual Prayer', p. 78.

11. *SAHG* B 14, ll. R6-14 (*HPD*, pp. 500-501; *Before the Muses*, III.4[a], ll. 62-72, pp. 242-43); B16; B 18, ll. 5-16 (*HPD*, pp. 176-77 [ll. 125-34]; *Before the Muses*, III.29, ll. 125-34, pp. 517-18); B 43, ll. 3-6 (*HPD*, pp. 169-70; *Before the Muses*, III.44[a], p. 585); B 44, ll. 4-8 (*HPD*, pp. 340-41); B 56, ll. 11-16 (*HPD*, pp. 403-404; *Before the Muses*, III.50[f], p. 638); B 61, ll. 45-50 (*HPD*, p. 191; *Before the Muses*, III.27[b], p. 507).

12. *SAHG* B 43 and 61, and pp. 395, 401; cf. Widengren, *Psalms of Lamentation*, p. 88; Hallo, 'Individual Prayer', p. 78.

13. *SAHG* B 47, ll. 40-44 (*HPD*, pp. 451-52); B 46, ll. 35-44 (*HPD*, p. 446; *Before the Muses*, III.44[b], pp. 589-90); B 56, ll. 21-40 (*HPD*, pp. 404-405; *Before the Muses*, III.50[f], p. 639); cf. B 40, l. 22 (*HPD*, p. 277); B 46, ll. 48-49 (*HPD*, p. 447); B 58, l. 11 (*HPD*, p. 393); cf. Widengren, *Psalms of Lamentation*, pp. 110-15, and for counter measures pp. 123-26.

14. Cf. Westermann, 'Struktur', p. 60 = *Forschung*, p. 284; *Praise and Lament*, p. 187: 'The Babylonian psalms at this point are much more explicit and concrete. They approach a kind of diagnosis.'

15. *SAHG* 45, ll. 1-10 (pp. 225-26; *HPD*, pp. 139-40); Widengren, *Psalms of Lamentation*, pp. 126-27; Dalglish, *Psalm Fifty-One*, pp. 25-26, notes that 'the role of the enemy is significantly small... The responsible cause is not the enemy but the offended deity.' Cf. for Israelite prayer D.R. Ap-Thomas, 'Some Notes on the Old Testament Attitude to Prayer', *SJT* 9 (1956), pp. 422-29 (424).

the enumeration of ills must also function as part of an appeal to the god, as it does in the prayers that are not connected with exorcism.[16] Otherwise the suppliant would hardly complain that his prayers have not been heard.[17]

In the biblical psalms, the attempt to prove the existence of magical ideas[18] has not met with general acceptance.[19] Certainly the explicit references which abound in the Babylonian exorcism series are entirely lacking in biblical prayers, and where the latter are given a narrative setting, for example, Hezekiah's prayer, there is no mention of exorcism. The long descriptions of sufferings are therefore to be understood wholly as elements in the appeal to Yahweh.[20] 'This description is in itself aimed at getting the prayer heard: it is intended to rouse the compassion of Yahweh and make him help'.[21]

Comparison with passages in the royal correspondence helps to indicate what their function is. Many letters describe the situation of the writer in the starkest terms.[22] The trouble may well be enemy action: the complaints in the Amarna letters about the activities of 'Abdi-aširta and his sons, and of Lab'ayu and the 'Apiru are well known and have already been mentioned. Rib-Hadda of Gubla (Byblos) writes as follows about the way his position is menaced by Abdi-aširta of Amurru:

> May the king, my lord, know that the war of Abdi-aširta against me is severe, and he has taken all my cities. Now only two towns remain to me, and even these he strives to take. Like a bird in a trap, so am I in Gubla (EA 78, ll. 7-16).[23]

(The image of a bird trapped in a net is one that is used in biblical prayers[24] and also possibly in Akkadian prayers.[25]) Assyrian officials also had to

---

16. *SAHG* B 13; 14; 17.

17. *SAHG* B 43, ll. 3-4 (*HPD*, p. 169; *Before the Muses*, III.44[a], p. 585); B 50, l. 14 (*HPD*, p. 313).

18. Mowinckel, *Psalmenstudien*. I. *Awän und die individuelle Klagepsalmen* (Videnskapsselskapets Skrifter II. Hist.-Filos. Klasse, 1921, 4; Oslo: Dybwad, 1921); Widengren, *Psalms of Lamentation*, pp. 238-50; N. Nicolsky, *Spuren magischer Formeln in den Psalmen* (BZAW, 46; Giessen: Alfred Töpelmann, 1927).

19. See Johnson, 'The Psalms', pp. 197-200; Ap-Thomas, 'Some Notes', p. 426.

20. Cf. Ap-Thomas, 'Some Notes', p. 425: 'The Israelite can seek to bring "moral pressure" to bear on his God by painting his own distress in the most sombre colours (Ps. 22.6, 15), or by pointing our the advantage to Yahweh of his deliverance (Ps. 35.17-18) or, of course, it may be the disadvantage to Yahweh of not rescuing him (Ps. 30.9)'; Gunkel and Begrich, *Einleitung*, §6.11.

21. Mowinckel, *Psalms*, I, pp. 196-97.

22. See also in the Old Testament 2 Sam. 14.7; 1 Kgs 1.18-19, 21; 2 Kgs 6.28-29.

23. Cf. EA 74, ll. 42-48; 79, ll. 34-37.

24. Pss. 35.7; 91.3; 124.7; 140.6 (EVV 5); 141.9.

25. *SAHG* B 13, l. I 43; *HPD*, p. 182 [l. I 51]; Widengren, *Psalms of Lamentation*, p. 123.

contend with enemy action, and described it vividly. An official in Syria, Uhati, reports that

> There is continual hostility (ND 2437, l. 40; *Nimrud Letters*, pp. 169-71; SAA 1, no. 176).

Nabû-balassu-iqbi, a Babylonian official, quotes to Aššurbanipal an earlier letter he had sent about the opposition he was encountering in Akkad:

> 'There are people here, my enemies, who are putting obstacles in my way— without the king knowing about it—and who say terrible things about me to the king so that the king should destroy me'. Your Majesty should know that the same two men who took the gold jewellery from around my neck still go on planning to destroy me and to ruin me, and what terrible words about me have they made reach the ears of Your Majesty! (ABL 716, ll. 25-R4; Oppenheim, *Letters*, No. 128).[26]

Like some of the psalmists,[27] a correspondent quotes the boasts of those who are guilty of lawless behaviour:

> When the king, my lord, had not yet stationed me in my post, they [the priests of Ea] used to commit thefts and cover them up. Left on their own, they can cover anything up without any effort, thus causing great whispering in the temple. Now they are all of one accord, saying, 'Let's do it this way'. I speak to them but they don't listen (SAA 13, No. 138, ll. R2-11).

Hostile words and actions are by no means the only trouble complained of. Mušezib-ilu explains why he has not been able to report to the king in person:

> I have been taken ill on the way; I am very sick;

and the scribe apparently confirms this:

> He cannot go. He cannot come into the presence of the king (ND 2387, ll. 5-7; *Nimrud Letters*, pp. 246-48).

Even those who did reach the king were not guaranteed a sympathetic reception:

> During my audience with my lord, I was not able to tell my lord about my misfortunes. 'Get out!' I was told. So I went, and on my honour I was not able to tell my lord anything (ARM XXVI.145, ll. 3-8 [*AEM*, I/1, pp. 309-10]).

Nergal-šarrani, a priestly functionary, writes to tell Esarhaddon that he is sick and appeals to him to send a physician or a conjurer:

---

26. Cf. ABL 942; 1241; ND 2681, ll. 5-10 (*Nimrud Letters*, pp. 63-64).
27. Pss. 12.5 (EVV 4); 35.21, 25; 40.16 (EVV 15); 59.8 (EVV 7); 64.6-7 (EVV 5-6); 70.4 (EVV 3); 71.11; 94.7.

Today it is a month since I have been ill and since this acute pain has been piercing me. They have pierced my…and jaw. I am being told: 'You are afflicted with "the hand of Venus", due to intercourse with women'. I am afraid. There is nothing I can do without the king's permission. Now, therefore, I am writing to the king, my lord. Let the word come forth from the mouth of the king that he should act and get me through this sickness of mine (ABL 203 [SAA 13, No. 73], ll. 7-R12).[28]

During the civil war between Aššurbanipal and his brother Šamaš-šumu-ukin in 652 BCE, the citizens of Ur complained that their loyalty to Assyria was putting them in danger of starvation:

We and Sin-tabni-usur (the governor of Ur) have kept the watch of the king my lord. In hunger [we] have eaten the flesh of our sons and daughters (ABL 1274, ll. 7-11).[29]

Others complain of shortage of water (ABL 327), shortage of oil (ARM XXVI.29, ll. R19-20 [*AEM*, I/1, p. 162]), houses in ruins (ABL 880), failure to bring in the harvest (ARM XXVI.31, ll. 34-36 [*AEM*, I/1, p. 164]) and hardships caused by bad weather (RS 20.33; *Ugaritica* V, p. 74).

Writers frequently complain of being slandered or falsely accused. Thus Rib-Hadda of Byblos writes to the pharaoh:

As to his having said before the king, 'There is a pestilence in the lands', the king, my lord, should not listen to the words of other men. There is no pestilence in the lands. It has been over for a long time (EA 362, ll. 45-53; Oppenheim, *Letters*, No. 75).

An Assyrian official, Aššur-da''inanni, had apparently been accused of disloyalty by another official:

I have approached the king my lord to say, there is no one who is not obedient. If I am guilty of an offence before the king my lord, let the king my lord kill me. But why should these people kill me?… Now that man has indeed been quick to send a message of calumny against me to the king my lord, when he said…that he sent me a message. We do our duty to the king my lord. Let that man and me argue it out eye to eye with the king (ND 2711, ll. 4-8, 38-44; *Nimrud Letters*, pp. 297-300).

An unknown Assyrian official had similar trouble:

The threat to my person about which I testified against them in the king's presence is the fact that they daily take an oath against me, saying, 'Let's kill

---

28.   Cf. ABL 327; EA 306, ll. 19-27 (cf. Moran, *Amarna Letters*, p. 344 n. 4); ARM I.115, ll. 11-19 (*DEPM*, I, p. 304 [No. 168]). In ABL 341 (SAA 16, no. 26), ll. 8-R2 Šamaš-metu-uballit asks Esarhaddon to send a physician to Babu-gamilat, a female servant who is ill.

29.   Cf. ABL 421 (*LAS*, No. 114; SAA 10, No. 173); 659; 756; 852; cf. ARM II.113, ll. 5-8, 17-29; V.25.

him!' But because they couldn't kill me, they are speaking to the king's magnates, their allies, and they are filing complaints against me before the king (ABL 1374 + other texts [SAA 13, No. 185], ll. 10-20).[30]

Several Assyrian officials complain about wrongful imprisonment: thus a priest in Nineveh writes:

> The chief victualler arrested and interrogated me without the authorisation of the king or the crown prince. He plundered my patrimony. All that my father had acquired under the king's aegis he plundered and carried off. (ABL 152 [SAA 13, No. 154], ll. 8-R2).[31]

Others complain of being out of favour, such as Adad-šumu-usur (ABL 2 [*LAS*, No. 121; SAA 10, No. 228]; 657 [*LAS*, No. 120; SAA 10, No. 224]) and Nabû-tabni-usur:

> (While) all my associates are happy, I am dying of a broken heart. I am treated as if I did not keep the watch of the king, my lord (ABL 525 [*LAS*, No. 264; SAA 10, No. 334], ll. R10-12).

Or the trouble may be that the writer's appeals or the king's orders are not getting through. This was particularly true, perhaps, when Sargon was away in Babylonia, and Sennacherib was left in charge at Kalhu (Nimrud). Nabü-usalla, an official in the extreme north, passes on the complaint of a deputation to Sargon:

> 'We spoke with the governor and the royal bodyguard, but they did not agree to bring us to the Palace' (ABL 206 [SAA 5, No. 104], ll. R7-11).[32]

Asqudum,[33] who took rather seriously the duty of informing on other officials, reports to Zimri-lim that a diviner is not receiving maintenance:

> When I arrived at Qattunân, he stated his grievance before me. The man has not received his maintenance. My lord has fixed the amount of his maintenance but Ilu-šu-nasir [the governor] has not given it to him (ARM XXVI.141, ll. 8-13 [*AEM*, I/1, p. 305]).

Others are impelled to write because of the importunity of the complainants:

> Šamaš-'înâin goes on about the field daily (ARM XXVI.146, l. 15 [*AEM*, I/1, p. 311]);

---

30. Cf. ARM XXVI.4, ll. 4-17 (*AEM*, I/1, p. 81).

31. Cf. ABL 390; 530, ll. R3-13.

32. Cf. ABL 238; 415 (SAA 16, No. 42); 733 (SAA 16, No. 98).

33. On Asqudum see Durand, *Archives Épistolaires de Mari*, I/1, pp. 3-6, 71-74. Another of Zimri-lim's officials, Bannum, describes him as 'an unscrupulous person... bent on evil...inspired by bad intentions...fundamentally hostile' (ARM XXVI.5, ll. 29, 33, 45 [*AEM*, I/1, p. 83]).

> The diviner does not stop complaining! He is very upset about the cost of redeeming the field. At present the diviner has calmed down (ARM XXVI.147, ll. 18-21 [*AEM*, I/1, p. 312]);

or because of the desperateness of the complainants' situation:

> The daughter of my lord, Kirû, who lives here, has said to me: 'Write and tell my lord that Hâya-sûmû no longer cares for me'. Now she has said to me, 'Because my lord no longer cares for me, either he will kill me, or else I will throw myself off the roof. That is what Kirû has said to me in no uncertain terms (ARM XXVI.304, ll. 37-46 [*AEM*, I/2, p. 60]).[34]

Yamsûm intercedes for Ibni-Addu, fearing for his safety at the hands of Hâya-sûmû:

> This man has been tied up inside his palace and taken to the town of Elali. Moreover, he has been imprisoned in a yoke and his house has been looted... At the moment I do not know whether this man is dead or alive. My lord should hold an enquiry about this man!... He is one of your loyal servants! You must not assume that he has committed an offence when it's a matter of life or death for him! Send a trustworthy man, a mounted man, who will be impartial, so that the man may live (ARM XXVI.312, ll. R7-9, 25-32 [*AEM*, I/2, p. 71]).

Plainly the main purpose of these passages in the letters is to inform the king just how serious the situation is. If only the king knows what is wrong, he will act. When someone like Rib-Hadda of Byblos sends repeated letters describing his situation, he is obviously not sending routine reports, but reminding the king of a situation he would prefer to forget, trying to move him by his importunity to take pity on him. Possibly none of the biblical psalmists thought he was telling Yahweh something he did not already know. But he would be haunted by the fear that Yahweh might have forgotten him:

> Will the Lord reject us for ever?
> Will he never show us favour again?
> Has his loyalty utterly ceased?
> Is his promise at an end for all time?
> Has God forgotten to show mercy?
> Has he shut up his compassion in anger? (Ps. 77.8-10 [EVV 7-9]).[35]

This fear would arise partly out of the fact that the distress continued, but also partly from experience of being forgotten by human authorities. The ordinary subject could be flung into prison and left there, or left to rot slowly

---

34. Cf. ARM X.33, l. 10.
35. Cf. Pss. 22.2-3 (EVV 1-2); 42.10 (EVV 9); 44.24-25 (EVV 23-24); also Aššurbani-pal's appeal to Marduk, captive in Assyria, to remember Babylon (Olmstead, *History of Assyria*, p. 405).

of disease, quite forgotten. The secular analogy did much to ensure that a moving account of the worshipper's sufferings should find its way into the prayers.[36]

36. Cf. Widengren, *Psalms of Lamentation*, pp. 230-34. Although he enumerates the calamities described in ABL as indicating the kind of calamities that underlie the Akkadian and Hebrew psalms, Widengren does not draw the conclusion that the psalms have been influenced by the secular situation. In his view any literary dependence is in the opposite direction: 'The phraseology is obviously borrowed from the psalms of lamentation. The very fact that they are so borrowed shows what sort of concrete instances and situations might be hidden behind these frequently stereotyped formulas' (p. 234).

5

APPEAL TO KING'S OR GOD'S OWN INTERESTS

The third motif common to prayers and letters is the argument that it is in God's or the king's own interests to help the suppliant.[1]

In the biblical prayers, the worshipper in distress has a claim on Yahweh because he is his servant—

> I am your servant, the son of your maidservant (Ps. 116.16; cf. 86.16; 143.12)—

or his anointed—

> But you have spurned and rejected me;
> You have been angry with your anointed one (Ps. 89.39 [EVV 38]; cf. 89.52 [EVV 51]).

Yahweh is reminded that his worshipper's enemies are his enemies:

> For see, your enemies are in turbulent mood,
> Those who hate you are asserting themselves.
> They plot cunningly against your people,
> And they scheme against your intimate friends.
> They say, 'Come, let us wipe them out, so that they are a nation no longer,
> So that the name Israel may be remembered no more'.
> For they have become of one mind,[2]
> And they are making a covenant against you (Ps. 83.3-6 [EVV 2-5]; cf. 5.11 [EVV 10]; 74.23).

Yahweh is also reminded that when Israel is defeated, his property is being defiled:

---

1.   Gunkel and Begrich, *Einleitung*, §§4.8, 10; 6.17; Clifford, *Psalms 1–72*, pp. 47-48: 'The psalmist urgently asks God: Will you, my divine patron, allow me, your loyal client, to suffer serious injury or death? The triumph of the enemies makes the patron God look ineffectual and uncaring. The client appeals to the patron's sense of *noblesse oblige* rather than to the client's own virtue. Rather than risk appearing ineffectual, so the psalmist reasons, God will act for the sake of the divine honour.'

2.   Reading יַחַד instead of יְחְדָּו.

> O God, the nations have invaded your inheritance:
> They have profaned your holy temple,
> They have reduced Jerusalem to ruins (Ps. 79.1; cf. 74.2, 7).

This motif is exceedingly common in prayers outside the Psalter, particularly from the post-exilic period.[3]

Again, when the man at the point of death reminds Yahweh that when he is dead he will not be able to worship him, besides the man's own sense of loss there may be a suggestion that it is in Yahweh's own interests to keep him alive, since only in this world is he able to testify to Yahweh's faithfulness:

> For Sheol cannot thank you,
> Death does not praise you,
> They that go down into the Pit cannot hope for your faithfulness.
> He who is alive—he can thank you
> As I do today.
> A father to his children
> Can make known your faithfulness (Isa. 38.18-19).[4]

Yahweh's kingdom is not regarded as beyond the reach of harm; it is not thought that disaster can make no inroads into it. It is bound up with the fortunes of a people, and the individual people alive in it, even though it does not owe its existence to their consent and is not at their disposal. Yahweh's rule will be discredited if he leaves his servants defenceless.[5]

The same themes are found in non-Israelite prayers. Ramesses II, in his prayer before the battle of Qadeš, demands of Amun: 'Has a father (ever) ignored his son?'[6] In the Egyptian prayer to Thoth found in Pap.Anastasi V.9.2-10.2, the suppliant prays: 'Come to me and care for me. I am a servant of your house.'[7] The suppliant's 'introduction of himself' in the *šu-illa*[8] may well have this aim of establishing his claim on the god's mercy. The quotation

---

3. Westermann, 'Struktur', p. 56 = *Forschung*, p. 279; *Praise and Lament*, p. 180; Exod. 32.11-13; Deut. 9.26, 29; Isa. 63.17-18; 64.10-11; Jer. 14.7-9, 21; Joel 2.17; Dan. 9.16-19; Neh. 1.10; 2 Chron. 20.11; Jdt. 9.8, 13; Add. Est. 13.15-17; 14.8-10; Sir. 36.12-19; Bar. 2.14-15; Pr. Azar. 11; 1 Macc. 3.51; *3 Macc.* 2.9, 14; 6.3.

4. Cf. Pss. 6.5-6 (EVV 4-5); 88.11-13 (EVV 10-12); Bar. 2.17; Gunkel and Begrich, *Einleitung*, §6.5; Mowinckel, *Psalms*, I, p. 237; II, p. 11; Westermann, *Praise and Lament*, pp. 155-59.

5. Gunkel and Begrich, *Einleitung*, §6.20; de Boer, *Voorbede*, p. 152; cf. Josh. 7.9.

6. Poem on the Battle of Qadeš, l. 92; B.G. Davies, *Inscriptions*, pp. 62-63.

7. A. Erman, *The Ancient Egyptians: A Sourcebook of their Writings* (trans. A.M. Blackman; New York: Harper & Row, 1966), p. 305; R.A. Caminos, *Late Egyptian Miscellanies* (Brown Egyptological Studies, 1; London: Oxford University Press, 1954), p. 232; Barucq, *L'expression*, p. 29.

8. Kunstmann, *Gebetsbeschwörung*, pp. 20-21; Dalglish, *Psalm Fifty-One*, p. 45; *SAHG* B 43, l. 16 (*HPD*, p. 170) ; B 44, ll. 3-4 (*HPD*, p. 340); B 46, l. 77 (*HPD*, p. 449); etc.

from Psalm 79 above is closely paralleled by this complaint in an Akkadian prayer:

> Eulmaš, your sanctuary, the foe has assailed,
> Your pure chamber he has defiled.
> In your pure place he set his foot,
> Your far-famed dwelling he destroyed (OECT, VI, 37, ll. 8-11; Widengren, *Psalms of Lamentation*, p. 169).

In another prayer, an *eršahunga* written in Sumerian, 'the enemies of the state are portrayed as having "made an end of your city", "destroyed the land", and "scattered the people of your land"'.[9] In the second plague prayer of Muršiliš, the king points out that, because of the plague, sacrifice is at a standstill, no one works the fields of the god, his name is falling into disrepute, and his reputation for justice is being lost.[10] The formula which concludes so many Akkadian prayers[11] has the same intention of arousing the deity to protect his interests: may he deliver his worshipper

> so that he may praise your divinity
> In all habitations continually glorify your great deeds.

The argument is used even more freely in letters. The official is himself a tangible part of the king's realm and ought therefore to be protected. Padiya, the prefect of Qadeš, writes thus to the king of Ugarit:

> Constantly to the nobles, my brothers, I have declared: 'The king of Ugarit is my master'. May my master therefore show favour to his servant! And may my master not abandon his servant! (RS 20.16, ll. 8-14; *Ugaritica*, V, p. 119).

Šarupši of Nuhašši is quoted in a treaty between his successor Tette and the Hittite king Suppiluliumaš as having cried

> 'I am the subject of the King of Hatti. Save me!' (*CTH* 53; *HDT*, No. 7, §1, p. 55)

when his country was invaded by the king of Mitanni.[12] The official is also the guardian of other parts of the king's realm:

> As I am a servant of the king and a dog of his house, I guard all Amurru for the king, my lord (EA 60, ll. 6-9)

is the claim made by the allegedly rebellious 'Abdi-Aširta.

---

9. Dalglish, *Psalm Fifty-One*, pp. 25-26; *HPD*, p. 148.

10. *CTH* 378; *ANET*, p. 396; *CoS*, I.60. The god's reputation for justice is invoked in terms very similar to those used in Gen. 18.23-25.

11. *SAHG* B 14, ll. R26-27 (*HPD*, p. 501); B 41, ll. 27-28 (*HPD*, p. 275); B 44, l. 17 (*HPD*, p. 340); B 45, l. 21 (*HPD*, p. 131); B 46, ll. 79-80 (*HPD*, p. 449); B 47, l. 78 (*HPD*, p. 453); B 50, l. 25 (*HPD*, p. 314); B 51, l. 31 (*HPD*, p. 316). Cf. Hallo, 'Individual Prayer', p. 81.

12. Cf. ABL 753, ll. R4-5; ARM V.66, ll. 21-23 (*DEPM*, I, pp. 203-204 [No. 77]); XIII.143 (*DEPM*, I, pp. 460-61 [No. 294]); RS 17.340. ll. 11-14 (*PRU*, IV, p. 49).

An official at Calah, appealing for resources, asks the crown prince who will look after the latter's interests if he does not:

> If only the crown prince, my lord, would turn his attention to me, I'd perform the works of the crown prince and deliver them to the crown prince, my lord. If I did not do it, who would do and deliver (them) to the crown prince? Would the accountant (and) the *drunks* do it? (ABL 885 [SAA 16, No. 34], ll. 22-R 2).

Correspondents remind the king that his property is in jeopardy. Rib-Hadda says of Gubla (Byblos):

> There is much property of the king in it, possessions of our ancestors in the past. If the king neglects the city, of all the cities of Canaan not one will be his (EA 137, ll. 74-76 [Oppenheim, *Letters*, No. 76]; cf. 286, ll. 35-38, 57-60).

There are two vivid illustrations of this motif in the Mari letters. Yasmah-Addu charges Šamši-Addu with neglecting his own property in forcible terms:

> Does the palace of Šubat-Šamaš really belong to another king? Or does the palace of Tuttul belong to another king? Both these palaces belong to Addâ (ARM I.118, ll. R21-23; *DEPM*, I, pp. 165-68 [No. 48]).

Halismu, king of Hansura, uses the same appeal very plainly in a letter to Zimri-lim, after he has reported that certain cities have been abandoned:

> These cities are yours! Do not be inactive and do what has to be done to liberate these cities! (ARM II.62, ll. 6-8; *DEPM*, I, pp. 484-86 [No. 307])[13]

The Old Testament yields one clear example of the secular use of this motif: Abigail persuaded David not to carry out his intention to kill Nabal, on the ground that when his fortunes are secure, as they surely will be, he will not want the enjoyment of them spoilt by the memory of a needless act of revenge (1 Sam. 25.30-31).

We may also note that a king occasionally admits the force of the appeal. In a letter to Kadašman-Enlil of Babylonia, Hattušiliš says of his vassal Bantešinna:

> Bantešinna is my subject. If he has cursed my brother, has he not cursed me too? (*CTH* 172; *HDT*, No. 23, §11, p. 142)

Once again, it is clear from these parallels that when the psalmists appealed to God to consider his own interests, they were using an argument familiar in secular life.

---

13. Cf. ARM XIII.143 (*DEPM*, I, pp. 475-78 [No. 303]).

6

QUOTATION OF ENEMY'S REPROACHES

A fourth common motif is the quotation of the enemy's reproaches.[1] If only the king (or Yahweh) can hear what the foreigners are saying about him, he will be stung into activity.[2]

Examples from the psalms are numerous:

> Remember this, that the enemy is taunting you, Yahweh,
> A barbarous people is treating your name with contempt (Ps. 74.18).[3]

Even the insults which the enemies hurl at the psalmist are quoted, since they are indirectly disparagements of the God he worships:

> I am a worm, not a man,
> Taunted by my fellows, despised by the people.
> All who see me mock me,
> They sneer and wag their heads—
> 'He depends on[4] Yahweh; let him save him,
> Let him deliver him, if he is pleased with him (Ps. 22.7-9 [EVV 6-8]).[5]

The argument from the enemy's reproaches is made particularly clear in Psalm 69. The psalmist has endured these insults for Yahweh's sake, as a good servant should, but he fears that other worshippers of Yahweh will be involved in his shame:

> Do not let your followers be shamed through me,
> O Lord, Yahweh of hosts;
> Do not let your worshippers be humiliated through me,
> O God of Israel.

---

1. Gunkel and Begrich, *Einleitung*, §§4.8; 6.8, 11, 28; 12.8; Westermann, 'Struktur', p. 56 = *Forschung*, p. 279; *Praise and Lament*, p. 180.

2. 'The citation of the enemies' words is a deft touch, a reminder that the enemies are attacking not only the psalmist but God as well' (Clifford, *Psalms 1–72*, p. 48).

3. Cf. Ps. 42.4, 11 (EVV 3, 10); 74.22-23; 79.4, 10, 12; Exod. 32.12; Num. 14.13-16; Deut. 9.28; Isa. 37.17 = 2 Kgs 19.16; Jer. 17.15; 20.8; Joel 2.17; Dan. 9.16; 3 *Macc.* 6.11.

4. Reading בל, third masculine singular perfect qal instead of imperative בל.

5. Cf. Pss. 13.4; 35.25-26; 44.14-17 (EVV 13-16); 71.10-11; 80.7 (EVV 6); 83.5, 13 (EVV 4, 12); 89.42, 51-52 (EVV 41, 50-51); 102.9 (EVV 8); 123.3-4; Lam. 1.21; 2.15-16; 3.46, 61-63; Add. Est. 14.11; 3 *Macc.* 2.17-18.

For I have endured taunts for your sake,
Humiliation has covered my face.
I am a stranger to my brothers,
An alien to my mother's children.
Zeal for your house has consumed me,
And the taunts of those who taunted you have fallen on me.
I bowed down[6] my soul with fasting,
And that brought taunts upon me;
I wore sackcloth,
And became an object of scorn to them.
Those who sit in the gate mock me,
And I am the subject of the songs of drunkards (Ps. 69.7-13 [EVV 6-12]).

There are no clear examples of this motif in non-Israelite prayers. This may be taken as an indication that the Israelite prayers are closer to the actual situation of the suppliant, and not so thoroughly adapted for cultic use as the non-Israelite psalms.

In the letters, the reproaches of the enemy are frequently quoted, but some caution is necessary before deciding the reason. First, quotation is a feature of the letters: what others say is given as direct quotation, and earlier correspondence is sometimes quoted in full. Then we have already seen that officials were duty bound to report any seditious words or acts: they were the 'eyes and ears of the king'. The reproaches would be reported in any case, not only to stir the king to activity. Nevertheless, it is clear enough that the enemy's malicious words are in many instances quoted to buttress the appeal for help. It is for this reason that Rib-Hadda quotes both the discontented grumblings of the people of Byblos:

Look, the people of Gubla keep writing, 'Where are the days when the king, your lord, used to write to you? Where are the troops of the days when they were sent to you?' (EA 138, ll. 122-26)

and the avowed intentions of the enemy:

They seek to capture Gubla, and they say, 'If we capture Gubla, we will be strong' (EA 362, ll. 23-27; Oppenheim, *Letters*, No. 75).

In a letter to Aššurbanipal's son Sin-šarru-iškun, Dadî, the chief treasurer, quotes the seditious words of Arbela in order that the king may confirm his authority:

I have now written to them as follows, 'Why do you not fear the king?' Ten men run around with them, draped with weapons, saying, 'Whoever comes against us we will cut down with (our) bows'. My lord, should c[all] his servants [to account] (ABL 727 [SAA 13, No. 20], ll. R4-14).

6. So LXX and Peshitta; Hebrew 'I wept'.

Issar-šuu-iqiša reports the disaffection of the Zikirtean chiefs to Sargon with a similar motive:

> Now let it be made very clear indeed to the chiefs. The chiefs have spoken insolently, saying, 'We have not heard in regard to [the governor]'. Let the king inquire of the second officer. He was present when the report was given to the commander-in-chief (ABL 205 [SAA 5, No. 169], ll. 14, R1-7).

Another official asks Aššurbanipal why such words are allowed:

> Why do Bel-šumu-iškun, the son of Sillaia, and Ša-Nabu-šu of Uruk speak, saying, 'In this house he is not faithful. Because you do not recognise Elam... Why have you established the base of the wall here? As long as you live, the land of Assyria will never love you' (ABL 1204, ll. R2-10).

This use of hostile words is especially clear when what is quoted is what the enemies *may* say if the king does not act. Thus Rib-Hadda writes to Amenophis III:

> Let it not be said in the days of the commissioners, 'The 'Apiru have taken the entire country!' Not so shall it be said in the days of the commissioners, or you will not be able to take it back (EA 83, ll. 16-20),

and 'Abdi-Heba of Jerusalem writes to Akhenaten:

> Let no man say in the presence of the king, my lord, that the land of the king, my lord, is lost, and all the regents are lost (EA 288, ll. 54-56; *ANET*, p. 489).[7]

Similarly, the governor of Nippur writes to the Assyrian king:

> The king should now send an order to Ubaru, the commander of Babylon, to grant us an outlet from Banitu-canal so that we can drink water with them from it and not have to desert the king on account of lack of water. They must not say everywhere: 'These are the inhabitants of Nippur who submitted to Assyria—and when they became sick and tired of the lack of water they deserted' (ABL 327, ll. R11-22; Oppenheim, *Letters*, No. 121).

---

7. Moran (*Amarna Letters*, p. 331) reads EA 288, ll. 54-56 as a denial that such losses have been reported: 'They have not reported to the king that the lands of my king, my lord, are lost and all the mayors are lost'.

7

DIRECT REPROACHES

Both in the prayers and in the letters, the suppliants feel free to turn to direct reproaches. If the duties of the subject towards the king or those of the worshipper towards God were felt to be clearly defined, a corresponding understanding of the king's duties towards his subjects and of the duties Yahweh recognised as his had been built up. It was therefore possible for a subject to charge a king with unworthy conduct, or laxness in the protection of his subjects. Similarly, it was possible to reproach Yahweh for allowing what was unjust to happen,[1] for neglecting what he had created,[2] for forgetting his oath and his covenant[3] and for not coming to his servants' aid, as he had shown himself willing and able to do in the past,[4] or as his quality of *ḥesed* implied that he would.[5]

In the psalms these reproaches find expression chiefly in 'the short reproachful question'.[6] These questions begin either 'Why?' (מַדּוּעַ, לָמָה), implying of course that the suffering seems to be undeserved,[7] or 'How long?' (עַד־מָה, עַד־מָתַי, עַד־אָנָה), implying that the distress is long drawn out.[8] Examples are numerous. A typical example of a 'Why?' question is

> Why do you stand so far away, Yahweh?
> Why do you hide in times of distress? (Ps. 10.1).[9]

---

1. Gen. 18.25; 20.4-5; Num. 16.22; 1 Kgs 17.20.
2. Isa. 64.8; Job 10.9.
3. Exod. 32.13; Deut. 9.27; Jer. 14.21; Ps. 74.20; *Pr. Azar.* 11-13; *3 Macc.* 6.15.
4. Pss. 25.6; 44.2-4 (EVV 1-3); 74.12-15; 77.6, 11-21 (EVV 5, 10-20); 89.50 (EVV 49); Judg. 6.13; Isa. 51.9-10; 63.15; *3 Macc.* 2.3-8; 6.4-8.
5. Pss. 6.5 (EVV 4); 25.6-7; 31.17 (EVV 16); 44.27 (EVV 26); 85.8 (EVV 7); 86.5, 15; 90.14; 119.76; 130.7; cf. Heiler, *Prayer*, pp. 240-41, 255.
6. Gunkel and Begrich, *Einleitung*, §§4.7; 6.11, 16.
7. Widengren, *Psalms of Lamentation*, p. 138.
8. Westermann, 'Struktur', pp. 53, 69 = *Forschung*, pp. 276, 294; *Praise and Lament*, pp. 177, 199.
9. Cf. Pss. 22.2 (EVV 1); 42.10 (EVV 9); 43.2; 44.24-25 (EVV 23-24); 74.1, 11; 79.10; 80.13 (EVV 12); 88.15 (EVV 14); Exod. 5.22; 32.11; Josh. 7.7; Judg. 6.13; 21.3; Isa. 58.3; 63.17; Jer. 12.1; 14.8-9, 19b; 20.18; Hab. 1.3, 13.

The following passage illustrates the 'How long?' questions:

> How long, Yahweh, will you utterly forget me?
> How long will you hide your face from me?
> How long shall I take counsel with myself
> And have sorrow in my heart all day long?
> How long shall my enemy triumph over me? (Ps. 13.2-3 [EVV 1-2]).[10]

These complaints can also take the form of statements about what Yahweh has done or permitted or failed to do, particularly in the communal laments:

> But now you have rejected us and humiliated us,
> And you do not set out with our armies;
> You have made us retreat before the foe,
> And our enemies have taken their plunder;
> You have given us up like sheep for food,
> And you have scattered us among the nations.
> You have sold your people cheaply,
> And you have not benefited from the price.
> You have made us the object of our neighbours' scorn,
> The butt and the laughingstock of those around us;
> You have made us a byword among the nations,
> Cause for the peoples to shake their heads (Ps. 44.10-15 [EVV 9-14]).[11]

These accusations against God belong to the earlier history of the lament: in post-exilic prayers they are replaced almost entirely by confessions of sin and affirmations of God's justice.[12]

Reproaches of this kind are also found in non-Israelite prayers. Before the battle of Qadeš Ramesses II asks: 'What is wrong with you, my father Amun?'[13] 'How long?' questions occur more frequently than in Israelite prayers,[14] in both the communal laments and the individual laments. In the former, Enlil, the god held responsible for the destruction of the cities in Sumer, is asked by Damgalnunna, the patron goddess, how long it will be before her city can be rebuilt:

---

10. Cf. Pss. 6.4 (EVV 3); 35.17; 74.10; 79.5; 80.5 (EVV 4); 89.47 (EVV 46); 90.13; Isa. 6.11; Hab. 1.2; Zech. 1.12. For questions different in form but similar in meaning, see Ps. 85.6 (EVV 5); Jer. 3.5.

11. Cf. Pss. 60.3-6 (EVV 1-4); 88.7-9, 16-19 (EVV 6-8, 15-18); 89.39-46 (EVV 38-46); Lam. 3.43-45 and *passim*. See Westermann, 'Struktur', pp. 53, 59 = *Forschung*, pp. 276, 283; *Praise and Lament*, pp. 177, 185.

12. See Westermann, 'Struktur', pp. 49, 71 = *Forschung*, pp. 271, 296; *Praise and Lament*, pp. 171, 202. Examples are Ezra 9; 1 Esd. 8.74-90; Dan. 9.4-19; Bar. 1.15–3.8; Tob. 3.2-6; *Pr. Azar.* 1-22; *Prayer of Manasseh*; *3 Macc.* 2.1-20; *Pss. Sol.* 9.

13. Poem on the Battle of Qadeš, l. 92; B.G. Davies, *Inscriptions*, pp. 62-63.

14. Westermann, 'Struktur', p. 53 = *Forschung*, p. 276; *Praise and Lament*, p. 177.

> When can I rebuild Eridu? How long must it remain destroyed? (Cohen,
> *Canonical Lamentations*, I, p. 85)[15]

The following is a typical example of the latter:

> How long, lady, have you laid this sickness, which does not cease, upon me?
> (*SAHG* B 14, l. R15 [*HPD*, p. 501; *Before the Muses*, III.4[a], l. 71, p. 243]).[16]

'Why?' questions, on the other hand, are rare:

> Why does the goring bull [Enlil] not rise up? (Cohen, *Canonical Lamenta-
> tions*, I, p. 397);

> Why are sickness, heartache, wasting away, and destruction, fixed to me?
> (*SAHG* B 17, l. 2).

The complaint 'Like one who does not fear god and goddess am I treated'[17]
occurs in wisdom literature as well.[18] The complaints here are stylised, however, and show little evidence of having grown out of particular situations.
An exception is the letter prayer Yasmah-addu addressed to the god Nergal
when the death of his son deprived him of a male heir:

> Why have you taken away my son? The kings who preceded me asked for an
> enlargement of the kingdom; I only asked for life and descendants. Do not
> envy those who are still alive! May the country not die away (ARM I.3, ll.
> R24-29 [*DEPM*, III, p. 72 (No. 931)]).

In the letters complaints are frequent and vigorous. Obsequiousness, which
might be thought to appear, for example, in some of the letters of Adad-šumu-
usur,[19] is rare, though the correspondent may feel it necessary to forestall
objections:

> Why have you thought it good to refuse me the oxen? Doubtless my lord has
> said to himself: 'If I give him yoke oxen today, when he comes, what will it be
> then? I will send it and he will make me give me another!' Doubtless, this

---

15. Cf. Cohen, *Canonical Lamentations*, I, pp. 59, 382, 395.

16. Cf. *HPD*, p. 183 (l. III 116); *Before the Muses*, III.31, p. 528 (the suppliant
complains that he has been kept waiting a whole year); *SAHG* B 17, l. 11; *SAHG* B 61,
ll. 56-59, 93-94 (*HPD*, pp. 191, 193); Widengren, *Psalms of Lamentation*, pp. 94, 106,
116; Gunkel and Begrich, *Einleitung*, §16 (p. 230 n. 6, ET p. 169).

17. *SAHG* B 14, l. R4 (*HPD*; p. 500); *SAHG* B 17, l. 12. Cf. *SAHG* B 61, l. 68
(*HPD*, p. 192; *Before the Muses*, III.27[b], p. 508). Widengren, *Psalms of Lamentation*,
pp. 179-81.

18. *Ludlul bel nemeqi* II, ll. 12-22 (*ANET*, pp. 434-35; *CoS* I.153 [p. 488]; Lambert,
Babylonian Wisdom Literature, pp. 10-11, 22, 38-39).

19. N.B. the adulation of ABL 2 (*LAS*, No. 121; SAA 10, No. 226) and the contrition
of ABL 620 (SAA 16, No. 36; if this is by Adad-šumu-usur; see n. above); also the wishes
for divine blessing on the king ABL 9 (*LAS*, No. 126; SAA 10, No. 218).

what my lord is thinking. Not at all, when I come to my lord, he will owe me nothing! (ARM XXVI.14, ll. R5-14 [*AEM*, I/1, p. 313]).

Usually, however, the reproach is delivered without apology. Bannum takes Zimri-lim to task for appointing Asqudum and his son to their posts:

How is it that you appoint as sheik of Hišamta a citizen of Ekallâtum? And how is it you have appointed Enlil-îpûs as major-domo? (ARM XXVI.5, ll. 20-22 [*AEM*, I/1, pp. 83-89]).

Albright speaks of the 'truculent tone' of Lab'ayu in an early letter (EA 252) to the Egyptian court;[20] but other correspondents are in their way equally forthright. In an early letter, Rib-Hadda complains to Amenophis III:

Why have you neglected your country? (EA 74, ll. 48-49).

Similarly, the inhabitants of Tunip complain that the pharaoh has failed to send Aki-Teššup with a chariot force:

Why does the king, our lord, call him back from the journey? (EA 59, ll. 19-20).

In the Assyrian letters the most frequent complaint is that letters have not been answered or that a plea has been ignored. Bel-ibni has sent captives and horses to Aššurbanipal but has received no reply (ABL 794). Aššur-resuwa writes to Sargon II:

Why is my lord silent (while) I wag my tail and run about like a dog? I have sent three letters to my lord. Why does my lord not consent to send an answer to my letter? (ABL 382 [SAA 15, No. 288], ll. 4-10).

Another official writes to Esarhaddon:

[Concerning the case of] Nabû-kabti-ahhešu [which I previously communica]ted to the king, my lord, why has the king, my lord, until now [nei]ther asked not enquired (about it)? Is it an insignificant matter? (ABL 1308 [SAA 16, No. 62], ll. 1-5).[21]

The citizens of Tunip had an even more discouraging record:

For twenty years we have gone on writing to the king, our lord, but our messengers have stayed on with the king, our lord... We have gone on writing to the king, our lord, the king of Egypt, for twenty years, and not a single word of our lord has reached us (EA 59, ll. 13-15, 43-46).[22]

Correspondents ask 'How long?' as well as 'Why?' Šarru-emuranni writes to Sargon:

    20. Albright, 'Amarna Letters', p. 104.
    21. Cf. ABL 1238 (SAA 16, No. 97), ll. R14-15.
    22. Cf. also ABL 542, ll. 6-8, 25; 740 (*LAS*, No. 258; SAA 10, No. 328); 839, ll. R7-8; 958, l. R17; 960, l. 4; 1114; EA 74, ll. 49-50; 137, ll. 71-72; ARM X.71, 179 (*DEPM*, III, pp. 297-300, 488 [Nos. 1115, 1257]).

I wait for the messenger of the king my lord, according as the king my lord speaks. How long is it to be until the king my lord shall speak to me, saying, 'Let the son of Bel-iddina go with you?' (ABL 311 [SAA 5, No. 199], ll. 5-9).[23]

The king may be reminded that it is his duty to protect his subjects, as by Nabû-ušabši and the elders of Uruk:

The king my lord should not forsake the kin of his servants (ABL 753, ll. 4-5).

Similarly, the ruler of Arzabia sends this message to Sargon for Sennacherib to pass on:

The ruler of Ukku must be kept away from me; why do you keep silent while he is trying to destroy me? (SAA 1, No. 29).

It may be added that in the Old Testament itself there are some examples of such reproaches of the king, and not only from prophets. Shimei even dares to curse the king (2 Sam. 16.5-8). Jonathan protests against his father's treatment of David:

He took his life in his hand when he killed the Philistine and Yahweh brought about a great victory for the whole of Israel. You witnessed it and you were glad. Now why will you wrong an innocent man and kill David for no reason?... Why should be die? What has he done? (1 Sam. 19.5; 20.32)

The woman of Tekoa turns her petition into a criticism of David's treatment of Absalom:

Why have you thought to do the same sort of thing against God's people? In giving this judgment the king pronounces himself a guilty man for not recalling the person he has banished (2 Sam. 14.13).

Joab can with equal force condemn David's unrestrained grief for Absalom:

Today you have disappointed all your servants, who have today saved your life and the lives of your sons and daughter, your wives and concubines, by loving those who hate you and hating those who love you. You have shown today that your leaders and servants mean nothing to you. I can see today that if Absalom were alive and we were all dead, you would be well pleased (2 Sam. 19.6-7 [EVV 5-6]).

It is therefore overwhelmingly probable that the freedom the psalmists use in reproaching Yahweh reflects the freedom subjects used in making complaints to the king. The theme is too stylised and conventional in the non-Israelite psalms for cultic inspiration to be a sufficient explanation.

---

23. Cf. ABL 604 (*LAS*, No. 34; SAA 10, No. 39), ll. 12-15; ARM X.68 (*DEPM*, III, p. 302 [No. 1121]).

8

EXPRESSIONS OF DEPENDENCE

In the psalms a sense of dependence on God is expressed, and in the letters similar terms are used for a sense of dependence on the king.[1] The motive is still that of persuading god or king to act, but not unnaturally the same expressions are sometimes found in laudatory inscriptions and hymns of praise, and it will be convenient to illustrate their use from these sources as well as from laments and appeals for help.

General Terms

We will first consider some quite general terms used to express this sense of dependence.

Trust

The psalmist frequently expresses his trust in God:

> Preserve my life, for I am loyal;
> My God, rescue your servant who trusts in you (Ps. 86.2).[2]

The same motif occurs in non-biblical prayers, such as this prayer to Enlil:

> My lord, I trust you, I praise you, my ears are inclined to you (*SAHG* B 41,
> ll. 17-18; *HPD*, pp. 274-75; *Before the Muses*, III.38[b], p. 558),[3]

and a prayer to Amun after the downfall of the heretical Amarna dynasty:

> Amun, I love you and I trust in you (Erman, *Ancient Egyptians*, p. 310;[4]
> Barucq, *L'expression*, p. 327).[5]

---

1. Heiler, *Prayer*, pp. 258-59.
2. Cf. Pss. 13.5; 25.2, etc.; Gunkel and Begrich, *Einleitung*, §§4.12; 6.19; Barucq, *L'expression*, p. 345.
3. See also *Before the Muses*, II.36, p. 156. Cf. Widengren, *Psalms of Lamentation*, p. 130.
4. A. Erman, *The Ancient Egyptians: A Sourcebook of their Writings* (New York: Harper & Row, 1966).
5. Akkadian personal names also express trust in the deity; cf. Widengren, *Psalms of Lamentation*, p. 80.

Such expressions of trust or confidence provide a further motivation for the deity to hear and answer the prayer.[6]

Letter writers similarly express their trust in the king. The king of Hanigalbat writes to the Hittite king:

> I have put my trust in Your Majesty, my father (*CTH* 179; *HDT*, No. 25, §3).

Raši-il writes thus to Esarhaddon:

> I am the one who blesses the king, my lord. I trust in the king, my lord. I pray to Marduk and Zarpanitu for the life, happiness, health, and longevity of the king, my lord. I must not become estranged from the king, my lord. Marduk-zeru-ibni is slandering me because he trusted Urdu-Nabû and Nadinu. I, on the other hand, trust in the king, my lord (ABL 498 [SAA 13, No. 174], ll. R1-11).

And a priest writes:

> He has silver at his disposal and trusts in his gold; but I trust in the king, my lord (ABL 555 [SAA 13, No. 45], ll. R7-10).

Waiting for God or King

Trust means, in practical terms, waiting for god or king to act. This is what is meant by the psalmists' declarations that they are waiting for God.[7]

> Let integrity and uprightness defend me,
> For I am waiting for you (Ps. 25.21);

> Guide me with your truth and teach me,
> For you are the God who will save me,
> I wait for you all the day long (Ps. 25.5);

> I wait for Yahweh, my soul waits,
> I expect his word (Ps. 130.5; cf. 27.14; 40 2 [EVV 1]).

This becomes even clearer against the background of the letters. Šarru-emuranni awaits orders from Sargon:

> I am waiting for the king my lord's messenger; what are the king my lord's orders? (ABL 311 [SAA 5, No. 199], ll. R5-10).

Urdu-Nabû, who is sick and cannot come to the king, writes to Esarhaddon:

> The king's servants are saying to me: 'Appeal to the king, go, get yourself cured'. I keep asking myself: 'How is the king, my lord, disposed? Nevertheless, I will appeal to [or, wait for] him'. Now let me not be lost to my lord. Let him appoint one exorcist and one physician to attend me. (ABL 1133 [SAA 13, No. 66], ll. R6-12).

---

6. Mowinckel, *Psalms*, I, p. 206.

7. It is possible that in some cases (e.g. Ps. 38.16 [EVV 15]) this should be understood as waiting for an oracle (Gunkel and Begrich, *Einleitung*, §6.4 [p. 178, ET p. 125]).

It is in response to an expectation of this kind that Aššurbanipal writes to Bel-ibni:

> You have informed [me], I shall act to the best of my ability (ABL 402, ll. R5-7).

Eyes Fixed on God or King

The psalmist may say that his eyes are fixed on Yahweh:

> My eyes are continually upon Yahweh
> For he will draw my feet out of the net (Ps. 25.15).[8]

The same motif is found, understandably enough, in Egyptian prayers to the sun, for example:

> You cross the sky
> (and) all faces are (turned) towards you,
> Unceasingly, (even) at night (N. de G. Davies, *Rock Tombs*, IV, No. 4; Barucq, *L'expression*, p. 27).

In the letters, subjects have their eyes fixed expectantly on the king. Thus in a letter to Esarhaddon in which the correspondent confesses an offence, he says:

> My heart, my arms, (and) my feet are placed beneath the chariot of the king, my lord. My eyes are constantly fixed upon the king, my lord, and the crown prince, my lord, constantly encourages me (ABL 620 [SAA 16, No. 36], ll. 7-11).[9]

This expression is also used with reference to the king in the Old Testament:

> Upon you, my lord the king, are the eyes of all Israel, that you should tell them who is to sit upon the throne of my lord the king after him (1 Kgs 1.20).

It is especially interesting for two reasons. First, keeping one's eyes turned to the king or suzerain is the attitude required by treaty obligation. Thus Muršiliš, in his treaty with Tuppi-Teššup of Amurru, says:

> You shall not turn your eyes to another. Your ancestors paid tribute to Egypt, [but] you [shall not pay it…] (*CTH* 62; *HDT*, No. 8, §5, p. 60).

Second, the analogy between the relationship with a human superior and that with God is made explicit in a psalm:

---

8. Cf. Pss. 104.27; 141.8; 145.15; Tob. 3.12.
9. Cf. ABL 2 (*LAS*, No. 121; SAA 10, No. 226), ll. 13-20; 412, ll. R13-16; EA 151, ll. 19-21.

See, as the eyes of servants
Look to the hand of their masters,
And as the eyes of a servant-girl
Look to the hand of her mistress,
So our eyes look to Yahweh our God
Until he has mercy on us (Ps. 123.2).

Protection

What do subjects and worshippers depend on king and god for? In the first place for protection. A number of expressions may be classified under this heading.

Protection in General

A letter shows that the protection of kings and gods can be thought of together:

> I always used to take refuge with Marduk and Zarpanitu. I always used to take refuge with the king, my lord (ABL 1034 [SAA 13, No. 182], ll. R4-6).

Tammaritu, the deposed king of Elam, says this in his reply to a kindly letter from Aššurbanipal:

> By the heart of the god and the protecting genius of the king he lives (Olmstead, *History of Assyria*, p. 463; ABL 943, ll. 5-6).

Zimri-lim implored the river god for protection:

> May my lord neglect nothing which concerns my protection! May my lord not turn his face elsewhere! May my lord not show his kindness to anyone else but me! (ARM XXVI.191, ll. 12-15 [*AEM*, I/1, p. 413])

The Hittite king Hattušiliš says of Ištar:

> I will take my refuge in God continually (*CTH* 85; Goetze, *Hethitische Texte*, I, p. 47).[10]

Esarhaddon received oracular assurances of protection from Ištar:

> I will protect my king. I will bring enemies in neckstocks and vassals with tribute before his feet (SAA 9, Oracle 2.5, ll. 23-25).[11]

---

10. A. Goetze, *Hattušiliš: der Bericht über seine Thronbesteigung nebst den Paralleltexten*, in F. Sommer (ed.), *Hethitische Texte in Umschrift* (Mitteilungen der Vorderasiatisch-Ägyptischen Gesellschaft 29.3 [1924]; Leipzig: J.C. Hinrichs, 1925), p. 47.

11. S. Parpola, *Assyrian Prophecies* (SAA, 9; Helsinki: Helsinki University Press, 1997). Cf. SAA 9, Oracles 2.2, ll. 16-19, p. 14; 2.3, ll. 6-10, p. 15; 2.4, ll. 16-17, p. 17; R. Borger, *Die Inschriften Asarhaddons, Königs von Assyrien* (AfO Beiheft, 9; Graz: E. Weidner, 1956), p. 16, Episode 11, cited SAA 9, p. lxxiv-lxxv.

The pharaohs of the Nineteenth Dynasty both claim the protection of Amun[12] and boast of their success in protecting Egypt[13] and their armies.[14] Ramesses II

> has protected Egypt with his wing, making a shadow for mankind, as a wall of bravery and strength (B.G. Davies, *Inscriptions*, p. 235).

The promise of protection is a vital part of treaty obligation. The treaty between Muršiliš II and Sunaššura of Kissuwadni contains the following clauses:

> As His Majesty protects his own person and land, he must likewise protect the land and person of Sunaššura... As Sunaššura protects his own land and person, he must likewise protect the person and land of His Majesty (*CTH* 41; *HDT*, No. 2, §§11, 12, pp. 19-20).[15]

The citizens of Babylon remind Aššurbanipal that among their chartered rights as a free city is the royal guarantee of protection:

> The kings our lords, from the time they ascended the throne, set their faces to protect our chartered rights and for our welfare, The kings our lords have ordained that those who occupy our fields, whether a woman of Elam, of Tabal, or of the Ahlamu, should have protection, as they have declared: 'The gods have given you open ears and an open heart. For all the lands is Babylon the bond of the lands; whoever enters there, his protection is guaranteed'. 'One breaking through the house of Babylon' is the name given to the charter. 'A dog which enters shall not be killed' (ABL 878, ll. 2-11; Olmstead, *History of Assyria*, p. 432).

Another letter consists of a proclamation of Aššurbanipal to the Babylonians as 'men under my protection', that is, citizens of an imperial free city (ABL 926, l. 1; Olmstead, *History of Assyria*, p. 476).

That mention of dependence on the king's protection is no mere convention is well illustrated by a letter from Rib-Hadda:

> Why does the king, my lord, write to me, 'Guard! Be on your guard!' With what shall I guard? With my enemies, or with my peasantry? Who would guard me? If the king guards his servant, then I will survive. But if the king does not guard me, who will guard me? (EA 112, ll. 7-18).

---

12. Ramesses II, Poem on the Battle of Qadeš, l. 171; B.G. Davies, *Egyptian Historical Inscriptions of the Nineteenth Dynasty* (Jonsered: Paul Aström, 1997), pp. 70-71.

13. Seti I; B.G. Davies, *Inscriptions*, pp. 3, 9, 15.

14. Ramesses II; B.G. Davies, *Inscriptions*, p. 57.

15. See also E. Golla, *Der Vertrag des Hattikönigs Mursil mit den König Sunassura von Kiswadna* (Breslau: Schlesische Volkszeitung, 1920).

Physical Defences
It is common to describe a god's protection in terms of physical defences. For example, in the Psalms:

> Yahweh is my rock and my stronghold and my deliverer,
> My God, my rocky cliff where I seek refuge,
> My shield, my horn of rescue, my secure retreat (Ps. 18.3 [EVV 2]).[16]

In Egypt the gods assure the pharaoh that they are his shield:

> My hand is a shield for your breast, averting evil from you (Medinet Habu 26.3-4; Edgerton and Wilson, *Historical Records*, p. 18[17])

says Amun-Re to Ramesses III.[18] In Assyria Ištar gives Esarhaddon a similar assurance:

> O Esarhaddon, I will be your good shield in Arbela (SAA 9, Oracle 1.6, l. 18, p. 8).

Akkadian proper names contain references to gods as bulwark, mountain, wall defence.[19]

Similar metaphors are used of the king's protection, particularly in Egypt. Abi-milku of Tyre writes as follows to Akhenaten:

> You are the Sun who comes forth over me, and a brazen wall set up for him, and because of the powerful arm I am at rest. I am confident (EA 147, ll. 52-56; Oppenheim, *Letters*, No. 67; *ANET*, p. 484).

Similarly, Ibašši-ilu writes to Esarhaddon:

> The king is the bulwark (lit. 'city wall') of the weak one (ABL 166 [SAA 16, No. 30], l. R 1).[20]

The metaphor of the wall has a long history in Egypt. A hymn to Sesotris III (Twelfth Dynasty; nineteenth century BCE) describes him as 'a rampart of walls of copper';[21] Amenophis II (Eighteeenth Dynasty; fifteenth century BCE)

16. Cf. Pss. 27.5; 61.3-4 (EVV 2-3); 62.3 (EVV 2); 91.1-2; Jer. 20.11; Barucq, *L'expression*, p. 346.
17. W.F. Edgerton and J.A. Wilson, *Historical Records of Ramses III* (Oriental Institute of the University of Chicago: Studies in Ancient Oriental Civilisation, 12; Chicago: University of Chicago Press, 1936).
18. Anat and Astarte are thought of in the same way: J. Černy, *Ancient Egyptian Religion* (London: Hutchinson, 1952; repr., Westport, CT: Greenwood Press, 1979), p. 126.
19. Widengren, *Psalms of Lamentation*, pp. 81-82; Noth, *Die israelitischen Personennamen*, p. 152.
20. Cf. ABL 1250 [SAA 16, no. 32], l. 15.
21. W.K. Simpson, *The Literature of Ancient Egypt* (New Haven: Yale University Press, 1973), p. 282; M. Lichtheim, *Ancient Egyptian Literature* (3 vols.; Berkeley: University of California Press, 1973), I, p. 199.

is 'a wall protecting Egypt';[22] Ramesses II (Nineteenth Dynasty; thirteenth century BCE) is 'a strong rampart around his army, their shield on the day of fighting';[23] Ramesses III (Twentieth Dynasty; twelfth century BCE) is called by his courtiers 'the wall that protects Egypt, so that they sit relying upon your strength'.[24]

Hand or Arm

Letter writers speak of the protection given by the mighty hand or arm of the king: 'Abdi-Heba of Jerusalem writes thus to Akhenaten:

> As far as I am concerned, neither my father nor my mother put me in this place, but the strong arm of the king brought me into my father's house (EA 286, ll. 9-13).[25]

They also speak of being grasped by or laying hold of the hand of the king. Thus Raši-il to Esarhaddon:

> The king, my lord, has reared me from my childhood until the present day, and ten times has the king, my lord, taken my hand and saved my life from my enemies (ABL 499 [SAA 10, No. 166], ll. 6-12);

and Adad-šumu-usur to Esarhaddon:

> Nobody has reminded (the king) about Urad-Gula, the servant of the king, my lord. He is dying of a broken heart, and is shattered from falling out of the hands of the king, my lord. The king, my lord, has revived many people (ABL 657 [*LAS*, No. 120; SAA 10, No. 224], ll. 16-R8; cf. Oppenheim, *Letters*, No. 95).[26]

The inhabitants of Tunip deplore the lack of the pharaoh's protection in the same terms:

> And now Tunip, your city, weeps, and its tears flow, and there is no grasping of our hand (EA 59, ll. 39-42).

The protection of the gods is spoken of in the same way, both in non-Israelite sources and in the Psalms. The Egyptian god Min 'gives his hand to him whom he loves',[27] and an Egyptian prays 'Give me your hand'.[28] An Akkadian hymn says of Ninurta

---

22. *ARE*, II, §792; B.G. Cumming, *Egyptian Historical Records of the Later Eighteenth Dynasty* (3 fascicles; Warminster: Aris & Phillips, 1982), I, p. 26, §1290.
23. Poem on the Battle of Qadeš, l. 12; B.G. Davies, *Inscriptions*, pp. 56-57.
24. Medinet Habu 23.1; Edgerton and Wilson, *Historical Records*, p. 15.
25. Cf. EA 288, ll. 13-15, 33-35; *ANET*, pp. 488-89.
26. Cf. ABL 876 (SAA 13, No. 147), ll. 9-13.
27. Barucq, *L'expression*, p. 239.
28. Barucq, *L'expression*, p. 373.

You grasp the hand of the weak
You raise him that is without strength (*SAHG* B 51, l. 11; *HPD*, p. 315; *Before the Muses*, III.47(b), p. 617);

Zimri-lim receives this assurance from Ištar:

With my powerful arms, I will keep close to your side (ARM XXVI.192, ll. 17-18 [*AEM*, I/1, p. 414]).

The expression used for assuming the kingship, 'seizing the hands of Bel', though it primarily indicated an act of fealty towards the god on the part of the king,[29] may also have implied that the king was putting himself under the god's protection.

This imagery is of course very familiar in the Old Testament. Yahweh delivers his people from Egypt 'with a mighty hand and an outstretched arm' (Deut. 26.8, etc.). From the Psalms we may quote the following from a communal lament:

For they did not occupy the land by means of their sword,
Nor did their arm give them victory:
But your right hand and your arm,
And the light of your face, because you showed them favour (Ps. 44.4 [EVV 3]).[30]

Shadow
Another very striking metaphor for protection is the shadow, whether this is thought of as the shadow of wings, the shadow of a rock or mountain or the shade of a tree. The shadow of various gods is referred to in Assyrian inscriptions, for example, in Sargon's Letter to Aššur:

Šamaš, the great judge of the gods, who opened the way and spread his protection over my army (*ARAB*, II, §176).[31]

Yahweh's shadow similarly is referred to in the Psalms:

He who lives in the hiding place of Elyon
And lodges under the shadow of Shaddai…
He will cover you with his pinions
And under his wings you will seek refuge (Ps. 91.1, 4).[32]

The king's shadow is mentioned more than once in the Old Testament: in Jotham's fable, with reference to Abimelech's attempt to make himself king of Israel:

29. Olmstead, *History of Assyria*, p. 181.
30. Cf. Pss. 17.7; 18.36 (EVV 35); 63.9 (EVV 8); 73.23; 89.14 (EVV 13); 138.7.
31. Cf. *ARAB*, I, §440; II, §§651, 702; I. Engnell, *Studies in Divine Kingship* (Uppsala: Almqvist & Wiksell, 1943), p. 193.
32. Cf. Pss. 17.8; 36.8 (EVV 7); 57.2 (EVV 1); 61.5 (EVV 4); 63.8 (EVV 7); 121.5; Isa. 25.4. See Gunkel, *Psalmen*, on Ps. 17.8.

> And the bramble said to the trees: 'If you are really going to anoint me as king over you, come and take refuge under my shadow (Judg. 9.15);

in a lament over the deposed and exiled king of Judah:

> The breath of our nostrils, the anointed of Yahweh
> Was captured in their pits,
> He of whom we said, 'Under his shadow
> We shall live among the nations' (Lam. 4.20);

and in Ezekiel's dirge for the Egyptian pharaoh, under the figure of a great cedar:

> All the birds of the air
> Made their nests in its branches;
> All the beasts of the field
> Bore their young under its boughs;
> All the great nations
> Made their home in its shadow (Ezek. 31.6; cf. 31.17).

In Egypt itself, Sesostris III is compared both to 'a cool place that lets every man sleep to daybreak' and to 'a shade in the inundation season, a cool place in summer'.[33] In Assyria, the king's shadow is referred to both in inscriptions and in letters. Building inscriptions frequently record that Sargon or a later king 'stretched his protecting shadow' over such and such a territory or city.[34] An oracle of Ištar says:

> Who is the man who had no friends, the man who is despised? Let him take courage under the shadow of Esarhaddon (Langdon, *Tammuz*, p. 139;[35] Olmstead, *History of Assyria*, p. 358).

In a letter found at Nimrud Sargon sends this message of encouragement to Sennacherib, who at that time had military duties on Assyria's northern frontier:

> Now eat your food and drink your water in the shadow of the king my lord. Let your heart be glad. There is indeed no reason for anxiety on account of the Muskaean (ND 2759, ll. R39-42; *Nimrud Letters*, pp. 188-92; cf. ND 2784; SAA 1, No. 1).

When Esarhaddon settled the succession, making Aššurbanipal king of Assyria and Šamaš-šumu-ukin king of Babylon, Adad-šumu-usur, his personal exorcist, urged him not to forget his other sons:

---

33. Simpson, *Literature*, p. 282; Lichtheim, *Literature*, I, p. 199.
34. *ARAB*, II, §§99, 104, 107, 117, 435, 957, 975; CH Epilogue, ll. Rxxiv, 40-49.
35. S. Langdon, *Tammuz and Ishtar* (Oxford: Clarendon Press, 1914).

Just as you have prepared a fine career for these sons of yours, prepare likewise a fine career for (the rest) of your numerous sons. Bring them into (your protective) shadow and shelter (ABL 595 [*LAS*, No. 129; SAA 10, No. 185], ll. 25-R1).[36]

A Babylonian official arranges protection for part of a tribe deserting from Mukin-zeri's rebellion against Assyria:

As for me, I have duly arranged settlement in the shadow of the king my lord. (ND 2636, ll. R9-10; *Nimrud Letters*, pp. 61-63).

Warrior

It is natural that the subject should depend on the king for protection, since one of the king's chief functions was to lead his people in war. 'We will have a king over us', say the Israelites to Samuel, 'to judge us, to rule us, to go out at our head, and to fight our battles—so that we may be like all the other nations' (1 Sam. 8.19-20). The king's prowess in war was one of the chief themes of praise.[37]

Yahweh is conceived as a warrior along very similar lines.[38] There is something of the hero or the champion about both. Compare, for example, this description by Esarhaddon of how he donned his armour before battle in Egypt—

I raged like a lion, I put on (my) coat of mail, (my) helmet, emblem of battle, I put on my head. I grasped in my hand the strong bow and the [mighty] arrow which Aššur, king of the gods had put into my hands (*ARAB*, II, §561)—

with the similar description of Yahweh:

Yahweh saw it, and it was wrong in his eyes,
That there should be no justice;
He saw that there was no man to put things right,
And was appalled that there was no one to intervene.
And so his own arm won victory for him,
And his own integrity, that upheld him.

36. Adad-šumu-usur is fond of this image of shadow or shelter: cf. ABL 358 (*LAS*, No. 122; SAA 10, No. 227), l. 14; 652 (*LAS*, No. 145; SAA 10, No. 207), ll. 18R9. Cf. Parpola, *LAS*, II, p. 108; A.L. Oppenheim, 'Assyriological Gleanings 4: The Shadow of the King', *BASOR* 107 (1947), pp. 7-11.

37. See the story of Sinuhe, ll. 34-77 (Erman, *Literature*, pp. 18-19; *ANET*, p. 19); the victories of Thutmose III (*ARE*, II, §§ 391-443; *ANET*, pp. 234-38); Shalmaneser I (*ARAB*, I, §113); cf. also Barucq, *L'expression*, pp. 246-47; Engnell, *Kingship*, pp. 185, 187-89.

38. See H. Fredriksson, *Jahwe als Krieger* (Lund: C.W.K. Gleerup, 1945); P.D. Miller, *The Divine Warrior in Early Israel* (Harvard Semitic Monographs, 5; Cambridge, MA: Harvard University Press, 1973).

He put on integrity like a coat of mail,
And the helmet of victory on his head;
He put on vengeance as a tunic,
He wrapped jealous anger round him like a cloak (Isa. 59.15b-17).

Again, Psalm 46 celebrates Yahweh's victory in terms very similar to those used in a hymn to Ramesses II. In the psalm, Yahweh

brings wars to an end throughout the earth;
He snaps the bow and cuts the spear in two;
Chariots he burns in the fire (Ps. 46.10 [EVV 9]),

while in fear of the pharaoh the Asiatics 'break their bows and are given over to the fire'.[39] As Yahweh's power in this respect is said to extend 'throughout the earth' (hardly 'throughout the land' merely), so Ramesses is said to reach 'the ends of the earth when seeking for battle'.

Provision

Protection is not the only thing for which people depend on God or king. They are also regarded as providing for their subjects or worshippers, providing either the necessities of life themselves or the conditions that ensure their supply. This is intimately connected with protection of course: it is the king's protection that makes normal life possible:

Didn't the king say to me as follows, 'Go, plant, fill the cellars with harvest and eat under my protection!'? (ABL 925 [SAA 17, No. 48], ll. 5-7).[40]

Giver of Life

Yahweh is naturally thought of as the giver and reviver of life:

Who keeps us alive
And does not allow our feet to slip (Ps. 66.9).[41]

The same is true of Egyptian and Mesopotamian gods, particularly of the sun god, Re, Amun-Re, or Aten:

Who gives life to every warm being
And to every good herd (*CoS*, I.25 [p. 37]; *ANET*, p. 365);

Those on earth come from your hand as you made them,
When you have dawned they live,

---

39. Erman, *Ancient Egyptians*, p. 259; K.A. Kitchen, *Poetry of Ancient Egypt* (Jonsered: Paul Aström, 1999), pp. 186-87.

40. Cf. ABL 886, ll. R1-4; the victory stele of Merneptah (Erman, *Literature*, p. 277; *DOTT*, p. 139; *ANET*, p. 377b); Kheti I (*ARE*, I, §404).

41. Cf. Pss. 80.19 (EVV 18); 138.7; 143.11; Jer. 14.22 (giver of rain).

When you set they die;
You yourself are lifetime, one lives by you (*CoS*, I.28 [p. 46]; *ANET*, p. 371).[42]

The Hittite gods 'give life' by sparing a person's life:

> When Tušratta, the king, died, Tešub gave a decision in favour of Artatama, and his son Artatama he spared (lit. 'caused the dead to live') (*CTH* 51; Luckenbill, 'Hittite Treaties and Letters', p. 165[43]).

But similar language is used of the king.[44] Even in the Old Testament he is described as 'the breath of our nostrils' (Lam. 4.20), and this is frequently paralleled in Egyptian sources. It is said of Amenophis II in the fifteenth century, 'There are no foreign lands which can build a boundary against him for they live by means of his breath';[45] and Libyan captives are still saying to Ramesses III in the twelfth century 'Give to us the breath, that we may breathe it, and the life, that which is in your hands!'[46]

Akkadian sources also provide more general language about the king as lifegiver. What is in mind is that the king has saved someone's life by sending a physician: Kudurru, the governor of Uruk, expresses his gratitude to Aššurbanipal:

> The physician Iqišâ, whom your majesty has sent to heal me, has indeed restored my health... I was about to die and your majesty has given me life! (ABL 274, ll. 12-13; Oppenheim, *Letters*, No. 93).[47]

Kudurru, son of Šamaš-ibni,[48] has been rescued by Esarhaddon from some kind of danger to his life:

> To the king, my lord: your servant Kudurru, son of Šamaš-ibni, a dead man whom the king revived... In the previous expedition the king, my lord, summoned me and raised me [from] the nether world (ABL 756 [SAA 16, No. 31], ll. 1-3, 6-8).

---

42. For Mesopotamian gods see C.G. Cumming, *Hymns of Praise*, pp. 61, 142; Widengren, *Psalms of Lamentation*, pp. 39-40, 49; Engnell, *Kingship*, pp. 191-93.

43. D.D. Luckenbill, 'Hittite Treaties and Letters', *AJSL* 37 (1920–21), pp. 161-211.

44. Gunkel and Begrich, *Einleitung*, §5.12.

45. *ARE*, II, §792; B.G. Cumming, *Historical Records*, I, p. 26, §1292.

46. Medinet Habu 26.18-20; Edgerton and Wilson, *Historical Records*, p. 19. See also *ARE*, II, §§804, 808, 819, 820, 891, 1032, 1033, 1037; B.G. Davies, *Inscriptions*, pp. 6-7, 14-15, 68-69, 82-83, 134-35; Medinet Habu 11.10, 11; 27/28.11, 12-13; 43.24-26, 27; Plate 78.17-18; Plate 95.24-25 (Edgerton and Wilson, *Historical Records*, pp. 3, 22, 45-46, 71, 101); Cyrus Cylinder R353; *ANET*, p. 316.

47. Cf. ABL 992, ll. R13-17; 501 (SAA 13, No. 173; 16, No. 127), l. 3. See also 2 Kgs 5.6-7 and C.R. North, 'The Religious Aspects of Hebrew Kingship', *ZAW* 50 (1932), pp. 8-38 (10-12); Barucq, *L'expression*, p. 249.

48. The two Kudurrus are distinguished in *Prosopography*, 2/I H-K, *s.v.* Kudurru, §§12, 20.

Or the king has made life worth living by showing favour: Bel-ibni acknowledges his restoration to favour by Aššurbanipal in these terms:

> With the many kindnesses, which from the first the king my lord has performed and bestowed, the king my lord has restored me to life, I who am but a dead dog, the son of a nobody (ABL 521, ll. 4-8).[49]

Or the king could make life worth living by sending an encouraging message or the help requested: Kumidu writes:

> May the king, my lord, welcome me and give me life, for I have neither horse nor chariot. May it please the king, my lord, to give life to his servant (EA 198, ll. 17-25).[50]

Royal inscriptions often express as much pride at having successfully provided for the people as they do in military victory. For example, in the Instruction of King Amenemhet I (twentieth century BCE) the king claimed:

> I was the one who made barley, the beloved of the grain-god. The Nile honoured me on every broad expanse. No one hungered in my years; no one thirsted therein (*ANET*, p. 419a).

Seti I 'nourishes the common folk',

> Filling the storehouses and widening the granaries, giving something to him who has nothing…
> There is no sleeping whilst hungry during his time, all the lands enjoying his food (B.G. Davies, *Inscriptions*, pp. 222-23).

Ramesses II is proud of the fact that

> Food is in his hands and affluence is beneath his feet,
> and provisions rest beneath his sandals (B.G. Davies, *Inscriptions*, pp. 122-23).

Much later, an inscription of Ramesses III says that 'supplies and provisions are abundant in his reign' (Medinet Habu 46.9; Edgerton and Wilson, *Historical Records*, p. 51). In Assyria, a cylinder commemorating the founding of Sargon's new capital at Dur-Šarrukin describes him as

> The sagacious king, full of kindness (words of grace), who gave his thought to the restoration of (towns) that had fallen to ruins, to bringing fields under cultivation, to the planting of orchards, who set his mind on raising crops on steep (high) slopes whereon no vegetation had flourished since the days of old; whose heart moved him to set our plants in waste areas where a plough was unknown in (all the days) of former kings, to make (these regions) ring with (the sound of) jubilation, to cause the springs of the plain to gush forth, to

---

49. Cf. ABL 657 [*LAS*, No. 120; SAA 10, No. 224], ll. 16-R8; 771, ll. 5-7; Prov. 16.15 (cf. vv. 10-15); Barucq, *L'expression*, pp. 248-49.

50. Quoted by Widengren, *Psalms of Lamentation*, p. 8; cf. the Punt reliefs (*ARE*, II, §257).

open ditches, to cause the waters of abundance to rise high, north and south like the waves of the sea…(in my time) for the wide land of Assyria, the choicest food, to repletion and revival of spirit (lit. 'heart'), as was befitting my reign, their (the gods') rain made plentiful; (there were) the choicest things to save from want and hunger (even) the beggar was not forced, through the spoiling of the wine, (to drink) what he did not want (what was not to his liking); there was no lack (lit. 'cessation') of grain of the heart's desire(?), that the oil of abundance which eases the muscles of men should not be too costly in my land, sesame was sold at the (same) price as (other) grain; that the feasts be richly provided with covers and vessels, befitting the table of god and king, the price of every article had its limit(s) fixed (*ARAB*, II, §119).[51]

On the other hand, the king might be held responsible for epidemics and famines: the stories of David's census (2 Sam. 24) and the siege of Samaria (2 Kgs 6.25-32a) in the Old Testament illustrate this.

Sun

This favourite epithet for the king probably belongs under the heading of the king as provider. It is especially frequent in the Amarna letters, where the king is both like the sun and 'is' the sun. For example, Rib-Hadda says to Akhenaten

Moreover, is it pleasing in the sight of the king, who is like Baal and Šamaš in the sky, that the sons of 'Abdi-Asirta do as they please? (EA 108, ll. 8-13).[52]

The Assyrian king Esarhaddon similarly is compared to the sun god (among other gods):

The king, the lord of the world, is the very image of Šamaš (ABL 5 [*LAS*, No. 143; SAA 10, No. 196], R 4-5).[53]

Abi-milku of Tyre, on the other hand, calls Akhenaten the sun or the sun god, the same word *šamaš* being used for both in Akkadian:

My lord is the Sun who comes forth over all lands day by day, according to the way of being of the Sun, his gracious father… You are the Sun who comes forth over me, and a brazen wall set up for him… I indeed said to the Sun, the father of the king, my lord, 'When shall I see the face of the king, my lord?' (EA 147, ll. 5-8, 52-54, 57-60; Oppenheim, *Letters*, No. 67; *ANET*, p. 484).[54]

---

51. Cf. *ARE*, I, §§407-408, 747-48 (Instruction of Sehetepibre; cf. Erman, *Literature*, p. 84); *ARAB*, I, §§249-54, 739; II, §435; Engnell, *Kingship*, pp. 191-93.

52. Cf. EA 149, ll. 6-7; 367, ll. 22-23 (Oppenheim, *Letters*, No. 64); *ARE*, II, §§269, 900; B.G. Davies, *Inscriptions*, pp. 4-5, 78-79, 122-23, 132-33.

53. Cf. ABL 633 + CT 53 426 (SAA 16, No. 63), l. 33; ABL 916 (SAA 16, No. 29), l. 14; SAA 9, Oracle 3.2, l. 7, p. 23. Interestingly, Adad-šumu-usur uses this as an argument to persuade the king not to stay indoors!

54. Cf. EA 319, ll. 19-23; 320, ll. 22-25; 323, ll. 17-23; 324, ll. 16-19; 325, ll. 20-22.

And in the Assyrian letters:

The king, my lord, is the sun (ABL 633 + K 11448, l. R33).[55]

The epithet is by no means confined to these collections of letters. Hammurabi is the 'sun of Babylon' (CH, Prologue, col. v.4);[56] the early Assyrian kings describe themselves as the 'Sun of all peoples';[57] in an oracle Aššur promises Esarhaddon that 'from sunrise to sunset there is no king equal to him; he shines as brilliantly as the sun';[58] the Hittite kings regularly take the title, 'the Sun, the Great King';[59] the inscriptions of Ramesses III refer to him as the sun.[60]

The analogy in prayer is obvious in Egyptian and Mesopotamian religion: prayers are regularly addressed to the sun (god) Re or Šamaš.[61] There is only one possible instance of Yahweh being described as 'sun' in the Old Testament (Ps. 84.12 [EVV 11]), but here the parallel 'shield' suggests that the correct translation may be 'battlement'.[62] Although the Israelite king is described as the 'lamp of Israel' (2 Sam. 21.17), the title 'sun' is never used of him in the Old Testament. Both the Egyptian pharaoh (EA 266, ll. 13-15) and Yahweh (Ps. 36.10 [EVV 9]) are, however, said to give light.

Shepherd
This is another title that expresses the idea of provider. Passages in the Old Testament in which this title is used of Yahweh are very familiar.[63] It is also used of the Israelite king:

---

55. At Mari there is one instance of a princess addressing Zimri-lim as 'my Sun', but his daughters regularly call him 'my Star' (ARM X.39 [*DEPM*, III, pp. 395-97]; B.F. Batto, *Studies on Women at Mari* [Baltimore: The Johns Hopkins University Press, 1974]).

56. Widengren, *Psalms of Lamentation*, pp. 10-11, thought that the concept of the king sun was Babylonian in origin.

57. *ARAB*, I, §§142, 159, 356, 437, 497, 596.

58. SAA 9, Oracle 3.2, ll. 5-7, p. 23.

59. Luckenbill, 'Hittite Treaties and Letters', p. 163 n. 1; RS 17.132, ll. 1-2 (*PRU*, IV, p. 35), etc.; Gurney, *The Hittites*, p. 64. Beckman, *HDT*, translates the title as 'My/Your Majesty, Great King'.

60. Medinet Habu 22.13-16; 23.3; 27/28.14-17, 72-75; 29.3-12; 35.14-15; 43.22; 46.6, 10; 75.6-7 (Edgerton and Wilson, *Historical Records*, pp. 13, 15, 22-23, 34, 35, 40, 45, 50-51, 65).

61. *ANET*, pp. 365-71, 386-89; Erman, *Literature*, pp. 138-40, 282-92, 307; *SAHG* B 4 (*HPD*, pp. 51-63); B 5 (*HPD*, pp. 63-66); B 53-58 (*HPD*, pp. 283-87, 364-65, 392-94, 403-405, 426-27); Engnell, *Kingship*, p. 183.

62. Cf. Akk. *šamšati*, and see Gunkel, *Die Psalmen, in loc.*

63. Gen. 48.15; Isa. 40.11; Jer. 31.10; Ezek. 34.12-16; Pss. 23; 80.

> I will set up over them a single shepherd, who shall feed them, that is, my servant David. He shall feed them and be their shepherd (Ezek. 34.23).[64]

It is used frequently of the king in Egyptian and particularly in Mesopotamian inscriptions: an inscription from Karnak describes Amenophis III as 'the good shepherd, vigilant for all people, whom the maker thereof has placed under his authority' (*ARE*, II, §900);[65] Sennacherib in his annals is 'shepherd...guardian of truth, lover of justice' (*ARAB*, II, §256).[66]

From time to time 'shepherd' is also used as a title for king or god in the non-biblical letters and prayers.[67] It is used of the Assyrian kings, as in this letter to Sargon II:

> May the king, my lord, the good shepherd, ...truly tend and shepherd them; May Aššur, Bel and Nabû add flocks to your flocks, give them to you, and enlarge your spacious fold; may the peoples of all the countries come into your presence! (SAA 1, No. 134, ll. 6-9)[68]

and of Šamaš:

> Whatever has breath you shepherd without exception,
> You are their keeper in upper and lower regions...
> Shepherd of that beneath, keeper of that above,
> You, Šamaš, direct, you are the light of everything (Hymn to Šamaš, ll. 25-26, 33-34).[69]

Patronage

Those who pray to the god and write to the king hope for patronage, as well as for protection and provision. In Assyria, and in Egypt under Akhenaten,

---

64. Cf. 2 Sam. 5.2; Ps. 78.70-72. See Mowinckel, *Psalms*, I, p. 56 and n. 43.

65. Cf. *ARE*, I, §502; J.A. Wilson, 'Egypt', in H. Frankfort, H.A. Frankfort, J.A. Wilson and T. Jacobsen, *Before Philosophy*, pp. 39-133 (88-89).

66. Cf. *ARAB*, I, §§113, 118, 125, 163, 180, 185, 217, 437; II, §344; S. Smith, 'The Practice of Kingship in Early Semitic Kingdoms', in S.H. Hooke (ed.), *Myth, Ritual and Kingship: Essays on the Theory and Practice of Kingship in the Ancient Near East and in Israel* (London: Oxford University Press, 1958), pp. 22-73 (27); McCarthy, *Treaty and Covenant*, p. 90; Olmstead, *History of Assyria*, p. 609; CH, Epilogue, Rxxiv, 40-45 (*ANET*, p. 178).

67. The Sumerian letter prayer cited by Hallo, 'Individual Prayer', p. 78: 'Like a sheep which has no faithful shepherd, I am without a faithful cowherd to watch over me'.

68. Cf. *Before the Muses*, III.4(a), l. 27, p. 241 (Aššurnasirpal I); III.4(b), l. 21, p. 244 IV.1(b), ll. R11, 15, p. 687 (an Assyrian king, of himself); IV.2(a4), p. 691 (Sargon II); IV.2 (a7), l. iv 19, p. 692 (Sargon II); IV.4(a), ll. 1, 40, pp. 697, 698 (Aššurbanipal); IV.4(e), p. 710 (Aššurbanipal).

69. W.G. Lambert, *Babylonian Wisdom Literature*, pp. 127, 129; *ANET*, pp. 387, 388; *SAHG* B 4; *HPD*, pp. 51-63; *Before the Muses*, III.32, pp. 532, 533. Cf. *Before the Muses*, III.27(b), l. 27, p. 506 (Ištar); III.38(c), l. 6, p. 560 (Enlil); III.50(c), l. 18, p. 657 (Šamaš).

there were no hereditary positions. All the offices of state were in the gift of the ruling monarch. Continuance in office as well as promotion depended on the royal favour.[70]

Mannu-ki-Libbali is at pains to assure Esarhaddon that he is not dependent on the patronage of anyone else:

> What have I been able to give to my lord in exchange for this favour that the king, my lord, has shown his servant? Would the patronage of the palace scribe have had such an influence over me that I would still be obliged to him? (ABL 211 [SAA 16, No. 78], ll. 8-11).

Rib-Hadda expresses the wish to be near the king:

> Moreover, it would please me if I were with you and so at peace (EA 116, ll. 48-50).

The reason is that the king provided for a circle of favoured subjects at court: the Old Testament provides many instances of this 'open hospitality'.[71] Yahweh is thought to hold court in much the same way. The following passage from a psalm must be read in the light of this system of patronage:

> How precious is your loyalty, O God!
> Men can take refuge under the shadow of your wings,
> They can take their fill from the abundance of your house,
> You let them drink from your river of delights.
> With you is the fountain of life,
> And by your light we shall see light (Ps. 36.8-10 [EVV 7-9]).[72]

Those who enjoy a standing at court are to be congratulated, as Solomon's courtiers are by the Queen of Sheba:

> Happy are your men,[73] happy these servants of yours who always stand before you and hear your wisdom! (1 Kgs 10.8).

---

70. Waterman, *Royal Correspondence*, IV, p. 22; Parpola, *LAS*, II, p. xviii; Barucq, *L'expression*, pp. 248-49; Hallo, 'Individual Prayer', p. 78; W.C. Hayes, 'Egypt: Internal Affairs from Tuthmosis I to the Death of Amenophis III', in I.E.S. Edwards, C.J. Gadd, N.G.L. Hammond and E. Sollenberger (eds.), *Cambridge Ancient History II.1: History of the Middle East and the Aegean Region c. 1800–1380 BC; II.2 History of the Middle East and the Aegean Region c 1380–1000 BC* (Cambridge: Cambridge University Press, 3rd edn, 1975), pp. 313-46 (353).

71. Gen. 40.20; 1 Sam. 20.5, 24-29; 25.36; 2 Sam. 9.7-12; 19.29, 34-36 (EVV 28, 33-35); 1 Kgs 1.9, 19, 25, 41; 2.7; 3.15; 5.2, 7 (EVV 4.22, 27); 18.19; 2 Kgs 25.29; Est. 1.3, 5; 2.18; Prov. 23.1-3; Dan. 1; Hos. 7.5.

72. Cf. Pss. 23.5-6; 27.4; 31.20-22 (EVV 19-21); 42.5 (EVV 4); 43.3-4; 65.5 (EVV 4); 73.17; 84.2-5 (EVV 1-4).

73. Hebrew אֲנָשֶׁיךָ; LXX reads οἱ γυναῖκές σου, 'your wives'.

Those who serve Yahweh in the temple precincts are likewise to be congratulated:

> Happy is the man whom you choose to approach you
> And to live in your courts (Ps. 65.5 [EVV 4]);

> Happy are they who live in your house,
> Who are always praising you (Ps. 84.5 [EVV 4]).

Ineni, a courtier of the sixteenth-century king Thutmose II, is in no doubt of his good fortune:

> I was a favourite of the king in his every place; greater was that which he did for me than those who preceded (me). I attained the old age of the revered, I possessed the favour of his majesty every day. I was supplied from the table of the king with bread of oblations for the king, beer likewise, meat, fat meat, vegetables, various fruits, honey, cakes, wine, oil. My necessities were apportioned in health and life, as his majesty himself said, for love of me (*ARE*, II, §117).

One of Amenophis III's architects, however, attributes his advancement in the king's service to the favour of the god Amun:

> My lord made me controller of your monuments,
> Because he knew my vigilance.
> I was a vigorous controller of your monuments,
> One who did right as you wished.
> For I knew you are content with right,
> You advance him who does it on earth.
> I did it and you advanced me (*CoS*, I.27 [p. 44]; *ANET*, pp. 367-68).

The man who cannot gain access to court feels left outside in the dark. Thus the governor of Barhalza, a province west of Nineveh, to Esarhaddon:

> Like sunshine, all the countries are illuminated by your light. But I have been left in darkness; no one brings me before the king (ABL 916 [SAA 16, No. 29], ll. 14-15).

Seeing (the Face)

An expression much used in this connection is 'seeing (the face of) god or king'.[74] Amarna correspondents express the desire to see the face of the pharaoh. Thus Abi-milku of Tyre:

> I indeed said to the Sun, the father of the king, my lord, 'When shall I see the face of the king, my lord?' (EA 147, ll. 57-60; *ANET*, p. 484; Oppenheim, *Letters*, No. 67),

---

74. Gunkel and Begrich, *Einleitung*, §§5.12; 6.4.

and Aziru, the son of 'Abdi-aširta, writing to an Egyptian official:

> What more do I seek? I seek the gracious face of the king, my lord (EA 166, ll. 6-8).

The pharaoh or the Assyrian king may invite subjects to come and see him in similar terms. Thus Akhenaten to Aziru:

> Come yourself, or send your son, and you will see the king at whose sight all lands live (EA 162, ll. 48-50);

Aššurbanipal to Nabû-ušabši

> Come now, in joy behold the face of the king your lord, and give him the counsel which is good for the king your lord (ABL 517, ll. R9-14);

and Aššurbanipal to the Gambulu tribe:

> Let Rimutu, of whom you spoke to me, come here, let him appear before me. and see my face, so that I can clothe him and do him honour. I want to encourage him and appoint him over you (ABL 293, ll. R1-7).

A letter from Nabû-šumur-iddina in Calah makes it clear that the image implies a personal audience:

> The face of the king, my lord, has been seen by very many people. Let an order be given to the palace overseers: when the elders pass by beneath the terrace, let them allow me to see the face of the king, my lord, and may the king look at me. Let them constantly send me word on the health of the king, my lord. Upon whom are my eyes fixed? In that I have written, let them allow me to enter before the king and speak to him (ABL 377 [SAA 13, No. 80], ll. 11-R9).

For the king to allow subjects to see him is in itself an act of patronage. Ramesses II compares his daily custom of hearing petitions with the rising of the sun each day—both are welcome:

> He shines in the horizon every day
> in order to hear all his petitions (which are addressed) to him.
> He says to him (every) time that he rises:
> What do you want? I will do it for you (B.G. Davies, *Inscriptions*, pp. 128-29).

For subjects, then, seeing the king is an opportunity to put a case in person, remove misunderstandings, and obviate the weariness of writing letters and getting no answer:

> [Once] or twice I have written to the king my lord, and I long [for] the sight of the king my lord, that I may see the face of the king my lord. Let him send a reply to my words (ABL 285, ll. R5-8).

So Bel-ibni to Aššurbanipal.[75] Even when the audience requested is simply for the purpose of making a report, permission cannot be taken for granted.[76] Aššur-šallimanni, who has victory over the rebellious Mukin-zeri to report, writes to Sargon:

> Let the king my lord, give audience to our messenger (ND 2385, ll. 13-14; *Nimrud Letters*, pp. 11, 45-46).

Sadly, being summoned to court was no guarantee of getting an audience:

> Unlike a servant of the king, on the day when I came here at the written order of the king, my lord, I did not even get an audience with the king, my lord. And I perish at my work, like a dog; I have not even entered the presence of the king, my lord. Am I not your servant? O king, my lord, let me behold that beautiful face of yours. Why must I die for want of food? Like a dog I bound about and roam around. I have no house, no maid, no servant. If this is the way the king, my lord, regards me, I am finished. O king, my lord, for what reason did you bring me here? (SAA 13, No. 190 [CT 53, 141], ll. R9-25).

Much has been written about the meaning of 'seeing (the face of) God' in the Old Testament,[77] and the parallel with 'seeing the face of the king' in the Old Testament[78] as well as in Akkadian letters has more than once been pointed out. In one interesting letter to Sargon, Aha-lurši welcomes the opportunity a visit to Babylon will give him to 'see' both the god Bel and the king:

> May Nabu and Marduk bless the king, my lord! that the king, my lord, invited me to Babylon, that I am going to see Bel and present a votive gift to Bel..., that I am going to see the face of the king, my lord, and kiss the ground before the king, my lord (ABL 842 [SAA 1, No. 132], ll. R7-12).[79]

75. Cf. ABL 740 (*LAS*, No. 258; SAA 10, No. 328), ll. R20-22; 604 (*LAS*, No. 34; SAA 10, No. 39), ll. 12-15; 757 (SAA 5, No. 47), ll. R1-4; EA 138, ll. 75-78; ND 2628, ll. 14-15; ND 2385, ll. 13-14; ND 2387, l. 7 (*Nimrud Letters*, pp. 30-31, 45-46, 246-48).

76. 'It was considered a great favour to be allowed to look at the king face to face—a favour mostly granted to those privileged to stay in the king's entourage' (Parpola, *LAS*, II, p. 208).

77. W.W. Baudissin, '"Gott schauen" in der alttestamentlichen Religion', *ARW* 18 (1915), pp. 173-239; E. Dhorme, 'L'emploi métaphorique des noms des parties du corps en hébreu et en akkadien. III. Le visage', *RB* 30 (1921), pp. 374-99; F. Nötscher, *'Das Angesicht Gottes schauen'* (Würzburg: C.J. Becker, 1924; repr., Darmstadt: Wissenschaftliches Buchgesellschaft, 1969); J. Reindl, *Das Angesicht Gottes im Spriachgebraush des Alten Testaments* (Erfurter Theologische Studien, 25; Leipzig: St Benno, 1970), pp. 147-63; A.S. van der Woude, 'פנים, *panîm*, Angesicht', in *THAT*, II, cols. 432-60.

78. Exod. 10.28-29; 2 Sam. 14.24, 28, 32-33; cf. 3.13; Gen. 32.21 (EVV 20); 43.3, 5.

79. Cf. ARM X.143 (*DEPM*, III, pp. 281-82 [No. 1099]); K.R. Veenhof, '"Seeing the face of God": The Use of Akkadian Parallels', *Akkadica* 94–95 (1995), pp. 33-37.

The parallel does not in itself decide what the worshipper saw or expected to
see when he approached Yahweh, but it suggests that what was literally seen
was not the most important consideration in either situation. 'Seeing the king'
was important because it meant audience and ultimately favour;[80] 'seeing
God' meant enjoying his patronage. Thus, when the psalmist says

> O God, you are my God: I will seek you earnestly;
> My soul thirsts for you, my flesh faints for you
> (In a parched, thirsty, waterless land[81])
> To see you as I saw you in the sanctuary,
> To see your strength and your glory (Ps. 63.2-3 [EVV 1-2]),[82]

the possibility of a visual experience is by no means excluded,[83] but it is clear
that something like a reversal of fortune is thought to be involved as well. In
Egypt the desire to see God is expressed almost exclusively with reference to
solar deities.[84] It is obviously a desire literally to see the sun, but for its life-
giving qualities as much as for its light and heat. In Akkadian prayers the
expression 'to see the face of the god' no doubt means that the worshipper
saw an image of the deity,[85] but even here the sight of the image symbolises
the opportunity to plead with the deity in person.

The case for thinking that 'seeing (the face of) God' has this idiomatic
sense is strengthened when it is remembered how many idioms there are
which include the face. A good Old Testament illustration is Gen. 32.21
(EVV 20):

> For he said, I will placate him (אֲכַפְּרָה פָנָיו, lit. 'I will cover [or wipe, smooth][86]
> his face') with the present which goes ahead of me; after that I will see his
> face (אֶרְאֶה פָנָיו); perhaps he will receive me (יִשָּׂא פָנָי, lit. 'lift up my face').

---

80. Nötscher, *Angesicht*, pp. 87-88; Reindl, *Angesicht*, p. 150; van der Woude, '*panîm*',
col. 442.

81. Or, with a few manuscripts and Peshitta, '*Like* a parched, thirsty, waterless land'.

82. Cf. Pss. 17.15; 42.2-3 (EVV 1-2; reading qal for niphal: see Baudissin, '"Gott
schauen"', pp. 181-84); Isa. 38.11 ('I said: I shall not see Yahweh in the land of the
living; I shall no longer set eyes on a man with the inhabitants of the world') is closely
paralleled by ABL 566, l. R11: '[May I not] perish. [May I] see the face of the king [my
lord] among the living'.

83. Widengren, *Psalms of Lamentation*, pp. 251-57, argues that 'the formula "see the
face of God" and "seek the face of God" ought to be considered traces of allusions to
images of the Israelite God' (p. 256).

84. Barucq, *L'expression*, pp. 396-98.

85. See *SAHG* B 51, l. 26 (*HPD*, p. 316 and n. 13); B 61, l. 41 (*HPD*, p. 190; *Before
the Muses*, III.27[b], p. 507); B 64, ll. 5, 8, 11 (*HPD*, pp. 457-58); Nötscher, *Angesicht*,
p. 73.

86. See G.R. Driver, 'Studies in the Vocabulary of the Old Testament V', *JTS* 34
(1933), pp. 33-44 (34-38).

In addition, Yahweh is said to 'hide his face'[87] and his face is said to 'shine' upon his people;[88] they may 'smooth' Yahweh's face[89] or rejoice in the light of his face.[90] The same expressions may be used in secular situations.[91] In every case it is clear that the literal sense is entirely subordinate to the idiomatic; what matters is Yahweh's anger and the appeasing of it, or his good pleasure and the enjoyment of it. An idiom of a similar kind which occurs both in the psalms and in the letters is 'lifting up the head' of the suppliant.[92]

Gifts of Land

The king's patronage sometimes took the form of gifts of land. When Samuel was telling the Israelites what kind of king they must expect, he said:

> He will take the best of your fields, your vineyards and your oliveyards and give them to his servants (1 Sam. 8.14).[93]

It is likely that when it is said that the Egyptian crown prince led Thutmose IV 'to pleasant ways' (*ARE*, II, §836), acquisition of territory is meant. The following lines from Psalm 16 may therefore have been composed with this form of patronage in mind:

> Yahweh is my share of inheritance and my cup;
> You wield my lot when I cast it;
> The measuring lines have fallen in pleasant places for me;
> Indeed, my property is excellent (Ps. 16.5-6).

In Loco Parentis

The king's patronage would have been especially important to any whose hopes of an inheritance from their parents had been disappointed. At Mari, Atrakatum, the wife of Sûmû-dabî, writes to Yasmah-addu:

---

87. Deut. 31.17-18; 32.20; 2 Chron. 30.9; Isa. 54.8; 59.2; 64.6 (EVV 7); Jer. 33.5; Ezek. 39.23-24, 29; Pss. 13.2 (EVV 1); 27.9, etc.; Reindl, *Angesicht*, pp. 91-109.

88. Pss. 31.17 (EVV 16); 67.2 (EVV 1); 80.4, 8, 20 (EVV 3, 7, 19); 119.135; Dan. 9.17; Num. 6.25-26; Reindl, *Angesicht*, pp. 127-37.

89. 1 Sam. 13.12; 1 Kgs 13.6; 2 Kgs 13.4; Jer. 26.19; Zech. 7.2; 8.21-22; Mal. 1.9; Dan. 9.13; Reindl, *Angesicht*, pp. 175-85.

90. Pss. 4.7 (EVV 6); 21.7 (EVV 6); 42.6 (EVV 5); 44.4 (EVV 3); 89.16 (EVV 15); Reindl, *Angesicht*, pp. 137-43.

91. 'Face shining': Prov. 16.15; ABL 463 (SAA 5, No. 260), ll. R11-12; Thompson, *Ancient Near Eastern Treaties*, p. 37. 'Smoothing the face': Prov. 19.6; Ps. 45.13 (EVV 12).

92. Ps. 27.6; cf. Ps. 3.4 (EVV 3); Gen. 40.13, 20; 2 Kgs 25.27 = Jer. 52.31; EA 144, ll. 14-18; ABL 954, ll. 6-R4.

93. Contrast Ezek. 46.18 and see I. Mendelsohn, 'Samuel's Denunciation of Kingship in the Light of the Akkadian Documents from Ugarit', *BASOR* 143 (1956), pp. 17-22.

> Given that neither my father nor my mother have left me a field or a garden as
> an inheritance, my lord must do what I ask of him. May he provide for me!...
> May he give me the means of irrigation! (ARM X.90 [*DEPM*, III, pp. 374-76
> (No. 1185)])

Zakir, the head shepherd of Nabu in Babylon, writes to Aššurbanipal as
follows:

> He has deprived me of my father's house, and he plays tricks on me constantly.
> May the king my lord not forsake me (ABL 416, ll. R4-7 [*CAD*, N 1,
> p. 155b]).

Sidqum-Lanasi, an influential citizen of Carchemish, asks Zimri-lim to treat
their new king, Yatar-Ami, as a father would his son:

> (Yatar-Ami says): 'My father Aplahanda is not dead; he is still living, since
> Zimri-lim acts as my father'. Yatar-Ami is a son for you, full of loyalty: guide
> him! And since his father is dead and he himself lacks experience, you should
> speak to him with no reserve (ARM XXVI.537, ll. R2-9 [*AEM*, I/2, p. 530]).

Rib-Hadda, writing to Amanappa, an official at court, asks him to say to the
pharaoh:

> You are father and lord to me, and to you I have turned (EA 73, ll. 35-38).

Adad-šumu-usur similarly speaks of Aššurbanipal as acting like a father:

> The king, my lord, has treated his servants as a father treats his sons; ever
> since mankind has existed, who is the king who has done such a favour to his
> servants, and what friend has returned a benefit in such a manner to his friend?
> (ABL 358 [*LAS*, No. 122], ll. 22-29).[94]

Sometimes the subject realises that he has received far more from the king
than he could ever have hoped for from his parents. It has already been
remarked that neither the rulers of Egypt under the Eighteenth Dynasty nor
the Assyrian kings relied upon hereditary office holders, but created a new
aristocracy of their own followers. Thus an official might say that at the start
of his career he was 'without (influential) kindred' or that he 'was humble of
family, one of small account in his town'.[95] The king therefore was 'he who
has built me, created me, caused me to exist' and caused him to take his place
'among men'.[96] Abdi-Heba of Jerusalem says explicitly that he owes his
position to the king and not to his parents:

> As far as I am concerned, neither my father not my mother put me in this
> place, but the strong arm of the king brought me into my father's house (EA
> 286, ll. 9-13; *ANET*, p. 487).[97]

94. See ABL 838, ll. 3-4.
95. Hayes, 'Egypt', p. 353; Barucq, *L'expression*, p. 384.
96. Barucq, *L'expression*, p. 248.
97. Cf. EA 287, ll. 25-28; 288, ll. 13-15 (*ANET*, p. 488).

The god is compared with father and mother in non-Israelite hymns, for example, in the Hittite prayer of Kantuzilis:

> [You], my god, [(are) father and mother] to me; [beside you there is no fa]ther or mother for me (*CTH* 373; *ANET*, p. 401),[98]

but the analogy is reflected rather more closely in Psalm 27—

> When my father and my mother forsake me
> Then Yahweh will take charge of me (Ps. 27.10)—

and in Gudea's complaint to the goddess Gatumdu among the Sumerian letter prayers:

> I have no mother—you are my mother;
> . I have no father—you are my father (Hallo, 'Individual Prayer', p. 78). ·

Similarly, Aššurbanipal says to the goddess Mullissu:

> I am your servant, Aššurbanipal, whom your hands created,
> whom without father and mother you brought up and raised to greatness (*CoS* I.144, ll. 16-17 [p. 475]).

Tokens of Approval

If it is impossible for the suppliant to attend the court, he may ask for some tokens of the king's approval. Padiya, the prefect of Qadeš, in a letter to the king of Ugarit, gives a long list of gifts which he has asked for and which the king has promised to send him, and then he adds:

> I have told my brothers: 'It is a great king who has taken (me into his service) and he gives me proof of his favour'. May my master then not shame me in front of my brothers. What my master is giving to his servant, may he give (indeed)! (RS 20.16, ll. 38-44; *Ugaritica*, V, p. 119).

Bel-ibni asks to receive insignia of office from Sennacherib, Sargon II's son and successor:

> Would that [your Majesty consider me again] one of his servants, that an official acknowledgment of my status as a servant of your Majesty come forth so that I will not be treated with contempt any more by my fellow Babylonians and will not have to [bow] my head in shame. If I see one such acknowledgment of your Majesty we will take new courage, and we all—I myself, my brothers, my sons, and my friends—we would go and kiss the feet of your Majesty and do service for your Majesty (ABL 793, ll. R9-19; Oppenheim, *Letters*, No. 90).[99]

---

98. Cf. C.G. Cumming, *Hymns of Praise*, p. 145; Widengren, *Psalms of Lamentation*, pp. 48, 276; Dalglish, *Psalm Fifty-One*, p. 44; Hallo, 'Individual Prayer', p. 78.

99. Bel-ibni's letter to the chief eunuch (ABL 283) is virtually identical; cf. also ABL 259, ll. R1-10.

With these examples we may compare such passages as:

> Give me a propitious sign,
> So that those who hate me may see it and be crestfallen.
> For you, Yahweh, have helped me and comforted me (Ps. 86.17);

> Our signs we do not see,
> There is no longer a prophet,
> There is no one among us who knows how long (Ps. 74.9).

There is a well known suggestion[100] that the transition from prayer to thanksgiving in certain psalms[101] is to be explained, not by assuming an inward conviction on the worshipper's part, but by predicating the intervention of some objective sign from God, such as an oracle, an omen or a dream. The desire that prayers should be answered in this way is clearly expressed in Zimri-lim's letter prayer to the river god—

> Now, I have just had brought to my lord a golden vase. Earlier, I had informed my lord and my lord had made me see a sign. May my lord make me obtain unreservedly the sign which he made me see! (ARM XXVI.191, ll. 5-9 [*AEM*, I/1, p. 413])—

and in the (second) Plague Prayer of Muršiliš II:

> If indeed it is for these reasons which I have mentioned that people are dying,—as soon as I set them right, let those that are still able to give sacrificial loaves and libations die no longer! If, on the other hand, people are dying for some other reason, either let me see it in a dream, or let it be found out by an oracle, or let a prophet declare it, or let all the priests find out by incubation whatever I suggest to them (*CTH* 378; *ANET*, p. 396; *CoS* I.60 [Second Prayer, p. 159]).[102]

The story of Saul and the witch of Endor shows that the same expectations were entertained in Israel:

> Saul consulted Yahweh, but Yahweh did not answer him, by dreams, by the sacred lot, or by prophets (1 Sam. 28.6).

The narrative in which Hezekiah's prayer is embedded includes the promise of recovery through the prophet (Isa. 38.4-6 = 2 Kgs 20.4-7), and this is supported by a miraculous sign Hezekiah asks for (2 Kgs 20.8-11; Isa. 38.7-8, 22). This strongly suggests that some tangible assurance was expected after a prayer had been offered, in the same way as the letter writer expected a reply and a token of support and confidence.

---

100. Gunkel and Begrich, *Einleitung*, §6.23.
101. Pss. 6; 22; 28; 31; 54; 56; 57; 61.
102. Cf. Prayer of Kantuzilis (*CTH* 373; *ANET*, p. 400).

The archives contain an occasional royal letter giving the desired promise of support. Aššurbanipal gives the following assurance to Sin-tabni-usur, the governor of Ur:

> Because I knew your loyalty, I have in turn conferred favour on you... The favours which I shall requite you shall be to children's children (ABL 290, ll. R4-6, 20-21).

We may compare with this the many oracles the Assyrian kings received from their gods. These might take one of two forms: either they would consist of favourable omens observed in the liver of a sheep,[103] or they might be put in the form of encouraging messages, such as the oracles from Ištar sent to Esarhaddon:

> [Esarh]addon, king of the lands, fear [not]!... I am the Great Lady, I am Ištar of Arbela, who cast your enemies before your feet... Could you not rely on the previous utterance which I spoke to you? Now you can rely on the later one too... You shall eat safe food and drink safe water, and you shall be safe in your palace. Your son and your grandson shall rule as kings on the lap of Ninurta (SAA 9, Oracles 1.1, ll. 4-5, 11-15, 1.10, ll. 6-12, 21-29, pp. 4, 10; cf. *ANET*, pp. 449-50).[104]

An inscription of Esarhaddon recounts how astronomical phenomena, 'messages from ecstatic prophets', and good omens in dreams and oracles combined to make him confident.[105] There is also a prayer of Aššurbanipal to Nabu which contains the answers of the god as well as the petitions of the king (*SAHG* B 39; *Before the Muses*, IV.4[f], pp. 712-13). Oracular elements in the psalms[106] and the encouraging oracles of the prophets (Haggai and Zechariah provide good examples) fulfil the same function.

Discomfiture of Enemies

Tokens of approval would have added value if they were public enough to discomfit the suppliant's enemies. The city Irqata writes to Akhenaten:

> May the king, our lord, heed the words of his loyal servants. May he grant a gift to his servants so that our enemies will see this and eat dirt (EA 100, ll. 31-36).[107]

---

103. See Oppenheim, *Ancient Mesopotamia*, pp. 214-215; F.H. Cryer, *Divination in Ancient Israel and its Near Eastern Environment* (JSOTSup, 142; Sheffield: Sheffield Academic Press, 1994), Chapter 3.

104. Cf. H.W.F. Saggs, *The Might that was Assyria* (London: Sidgwick & Jackson, 1984), p. 275; on the relationship of the Assyrian kings to Ištar see Oppenheim, *Ancient Mesopotamia*, pp. 205-206.

105. Borger, *Asarhaddon*, Ass. A, ll. i.31–ii.11, p. 2 (SAA 9, p. lxxiv).

106. See Johnson, 'The Psalms', pp. 177-80, 205-206; Mowinckel, *Psalms*, II, pp. 53-73.

107. Moran, *Amarna Letters*, p. 173 n. 8: '"To eat dirt" means "to be defeated"' (*CAD*, A.1, p. 256).

The psalmist prays:

> You prepare a meal for me
> In front of my enemies (Ps. 23.5).[108]

Promise that his enemies will be vanquished is a feature of the oracles addressed to Esarhaddon:

> Your enemies will roll before your feet like ripe apples... I will flay your enemies and give them to you (SAA 9, Oracle 1.1, ll. 8-10, 18-19, p. 4).[109]

Counsel

Letters are written, not only to elicit encouragement and tokens of approval, but also specific directions in particular circumstances. Hence correspondents frequently say how much they value the king's counsel. Aziru, the son of 'Abdi-Asirta, writes as follows to Tutu, a high official of Akhenaten:

> Hatip has come and brought the gracious and sweet words of the king, my lord, and I am quite overjoyed. My land and my brothers, the servants of the king, my lord, and the servants of Tutu, my lord, are overjoyed when the breath of the king, my lord, comes. I do not deviate from the orders of my lord, my god, my Sun, and from the orders of Tutu, my lord (EA 164, ll. 4-17).

The king has been endowed with wisdom by the gods:

> Bel and Nabu have given vast insight to the king, my lord (ABL 211 [SAA 16, No. 78], ll. 13-14).

The king's decisions, and even those of the queen mother,[110] are final:

> The word of the king, my lord, is just as final as that of the gods (ABL 1221 [SAA 13, No. 46], ll. 11-12).

They defer to it against their better judgment: a letter from Nimrud contains the following:

> If the king my lord should say: 'Let them take and eat for themselves', then let them take and eat; the king my lord certainly knows best (ND 2766, ll. R 5-9; *Nimrud Letters*, pp. 161-63).

In another Nimrud letter an official who pleads that he cannot carry out the king's orders finds it prudent to disarm a possible rebuke by quoting what

---

108. Cf. Ps. 86.17.

109. Cf. SAA 9, Oracles 1.1, ll. 11-15, p. 4; 1.6, ll. 7-10, p. 8; 2.3, ll. 6-10, p. 15; 2.5, ll. 23-25, p. 16; Borger, *Asarhaddon*, Nin. A, ll. i.59-62 (SAA 9, p. lxxiii).

110. See *LAS*, No. 230, l. R1. In the queen mother's case, it is the effectiveness of her curses and blessings which is being asserted: 'What you bless, is blessed. What you curse, is cursed.'

may be a proverbial saying: 'He who answered the king back died' (ND 2771, ll. 11-12; *Nimrud Letters*, pp. 312-13).[111]

Similarly, worshippers look to the gods for advice. A hymn from the First Dynasty of Babylon says of Ištar:

> With this goddess there is counsel.
> The fate of everything she holds in her hand (*ANET*, p. 383; *SAHG* B 1, ll. 13-14; *HPD*, p. 39; *Before the Muses*, II.1, p. 69).

In the Neo-Assyrian period queries were regularly addressed to Šamaš.[112]

The advice may first of all be given to the other gods. They seek the advice of Sin, for example:

> The great gods inquire of you and you give them advice (*SAHG* B 52, l. 14; *HPD*, p. 278; *Before the Muses*, III.52[b], p. 667).

Marduk is imagined acting in a similar capacity.[113] The advice reaches human beings through divination and oracles.[114]

So in Israel:

> I will bless Yahweh, who has advised me (Ps. 16.7).[115]

This would often be the result of consulting God at a sanctuary and receiving an oracle in reply.[116] The praise of Yahweh for his word and his law is a development of this gratitude for good advice.[117]

Hyperbolic Expressions

We may conclude this section on expressions of dependence by noticing that certain hyperbolic expressions are used of king and god alike.

No One Else

The king's help is indispensable. Without the king the subject can do nothing, either about sickness or about conquest. Nergal-šarrani appeals to Esarhaddon to send a physician or conjurer to cure him:

111. On 'counsel' in the Hebrew Bible, see J. Pedersen, *Israel: Its Life and Culture*, I-II (London: Oxford University Press; Copenhagen: Branner & Korch, 1926), pp. 128-30.

112. I. Starr, *Queries to the Sungod: Divination and Politics in Sargonid Assyria* (SAA, 4; Helsinki: Helsinki University Press, 1990).

113. *SAHG* B 6, ll. 26-28; *HPD*, p. 118; *Before the Muses*, IV.4(d), p. 706.

114. C.G. Cumming, *Hymns of Praise*, p. 133; *Before the Muses*, p. 665.

115. Cf. Pss. 73.24; 139.17.

116. J. Pedersen, *Israel: Its Life and Culture*, III-IV (London: Oxford University Press; Copenhagen: Branner & Korch, 1940), p. 455.

117. Pss. 19.8 (EVV 7); 138.2, 4; Jer. 15.16; cf. C.G. Cumming, *Hymns of Praise*, pp. 69, 89-91, 127-29; Olmstead, *History of Assyria*, p. 367.

Today it is a month since I have been ill and since this acute pain has been piercing me. They have pierced my...and jaw. I am being told: 'You are afflicted with "the hand of Venus", due to intercourse with women'. I am afraid. There is nothing I can do without the king's permission. Now, therefore, I am writing to the king, my lord. Let the word come forth from the mouth of the king that he should act and get me through this sickness of mine (ABL 203 [SAA 13, No. 73], ll. 7-R12).

Correspondents frequently say that there is no one else to turn to. Rib-Hadda insists that there is no one but the pharaoh himself to defend Byblos:

If they capture Gubla, they will be strong; there will not be a man left, and they (the archers) will certainly be too few for them... Should I move to the outlying territory, then the men will desert in order to take territory for themselves, and there will be no men to guard Gubla, the city of the king, my lord (EA 362, ll. 27-30, 33-39; Oppenheim, *Letters*, No. 75).

Adad-šumu-uṣur says that he has no patron but the king:

My eyes are fixed on the king, my lord. None of those who stay in the palace like me; there is not a single friend of mine among them, to whom I would give a present, who would accept it and speak for me. May the king, my lord, have mercy on his servant. (ABL 2 [*LAS*, No. 121], ll. R13-20; Oppenheim, *Letters*, No. 86).[118]

These passages are reminiscent of several in the psalms:

Whom have I in heaven? (Ps. 73.25);

I looked to the right and saw,
And there was no one who would recognise me:
My refuge is destroyed;
No one looks after me (Ps. 142.5 [EVV 4]).[119]

Incomparable

Both king and god are described as incomparable. We may recall Adad-šumu-uṣur's praise of Aššurbanipal already quoted.[120] Aha-lurši tells Sargon that his deeds are far superior to those of his predecessors:

Verily, [by Bel and Nabu, your gods,] there are no works done [under] your royal forefathers that can be compared to those [done] in the reign of the king, my lord! (ABL 841 [SAA 1, No. 132], ll. 14-16).

---

118. Cf. ABL 206 (SAA 5, No. 104), ll. R1-11; 733, l. R6; 1149 (SAA 13, No. 158), ll. R4-11; 968 (SAA 13, No. 179), l. 4; SAA 13, No. 178, ll. R21-25 (cf. B. Landsberger, *Brief des Bischofs von Esagila an König Asarhaddon* [Amsterdam: Noord-Hollandsche Uitgevers-Maatschappij, 1965]); ARM V, 5, ll. 12-15.
    119. Cf. Isa. 63.5; Add. Est. 14.3.
    120. ABL 358 (*LAS*, No. 122); Engnell, *Kingship*, p. 179.

An oracle declares of Esarhaddon:

> From sunrise to sunset there is no king equal to him; he shines as brilliantly as
> the sun (SAA 9, Oracle 3.2, l. 7, p. 23).

The pharaoh, similarly, is a 'brave warrior without match', a 'bowman without equal'.[121] There is, however, an awareness that this may be pardonable exaggeration:

> Strong King of whom one boasts;
> Sovereign of whom one exaggerates (B.G. Davies, *Inscriptions*, pp. 48-49).

The theme is common in Akkadian hymns:

> Who—to her greatness who can be equal?
> Strong, exalted, splendid are her decrees.
> Istar—to her greatness who can be equal?
> Strong, exalted, splendid are her decrees (*ANET*, p. 383 [*SAHG* B 1, ll. 21-24;
> *HPD*, p. 40; *Before the Muses*, II.1(vi), p. 69]).[122]

It is found also in Egypt:

> O my God, Lord of the Gods,
> Amen-Re, Lord of the Thrones of the Two Lands!
> Give me a hand, deliver me,
> shine forth for me, may you enable me to live;
> You are the unique God, unequalled (Berlin 6910 H.6-7; Kitchen, *Poetry*,
> pp. 274-75).[123]

Yahweh is praised in similar terms in the Old Testament:

> Who is like you among the gods, Yahweh?
> Who is like you, majestic in holiness,
> Inspiring reverent praise, performing wonderful deeds? (Exod. 15.11).[124]

To the Ends of the Earth
A passage which has often been cited as an important parallel with the Old Testament is the following, from a letter written by Tagi, who held territory on the coastal plain just south of Mt Carmel in the Amarna age:

> Should we go up into the sky, or should we go down into the netherworld, our
> head is in your hand (EA 264, ll. 15-19; Oppenheim, *Letters*, No. 71).

---

121. B.G. Davies, *Inscriptions*, pp. 14-15, 56-57.
122. Cf. a hymn to the moon god (*ANET*, p. 386); C.G. Cumming, *Hymns of Praise*, pp. 56, 73, 76, 103.
123. Cf. Barucq, *L'expression*, p. 179.
124. Cf. Deut. 3.24; 1 Sam. 2.2; 2 Sam. 7.22; 1 Kgs 8.23 = 2 Chron. 6.14; Pss. 35.10; 71.19; 86.8; 89.7 (EVV 6); 113.5-6; Jer. 10.6.

The comparison is with Ps. 139.7-10:

> Where shall I go away from your spirit?
> Where shall I escape from your presence?
> If I go up to heaven, you are there:
> If I spread out my couch in Sheol, there you are too.
> And if I take up the wings of dawn
> And go and live at the furthest parts of the sea,
> Even there your hand will guide me,
> And your right hand will hold me.

Just as Yahweh's activity extends to the ends of the earth,[125] so does that of the Assyrian or Egyptian king. Adad-šumu-usur writes to Esarhaddon:

> Now, O king, my lord, the god Aššur has given you the world from the rising of the sun to the setting of the sun (*LAS* 129, ll. R17-18).

Ubaru, newly appointed governor of Babylon, reports to Esarhaddon:

> All the lands are happy before the king my lord (ABL 418 [SAA 18, No. 14], ll. R10-13).[126]

Akhenaten is regarded as receiving universal homage:

> The South as the North, the West and the East, the islands which are in the middle of the sea acclaim your *ka* (N. de G. Davies, *Rock Tombs*, III, No. 29, ll. 5-6).[127]

One correspondent, possibly Adad-šumu-usur, mentions a song of Akkad which says of the king:

> Who does not love his benefactor? In a song from Babylonia it is said: 'On account of your good words, O my shepherd, all the masters look forward to you' (ABL 435 [*LAS*, No. 124], ll. R9-14; Oppenheim, *Letters*, No. 89).

Under Surveillance

All that people do has Yahweh's attention:

> Yahweh looks from heaven
> And sees all the human race.
> From the place where he lives he gazes
> On all the inhabitants of the earth,
> He who forms the hearts of them all
> And attends to all that they do (Ps. 33.13-15).

The same is said of Šamaš:

---

125. Pss. 22.28 (evv 27); 65.6 (evv 5); 67.8 (evv 7); 72.11; 86.9.

126. Cf. ABL 435 (*LAS*, No. 124), ll. 3-10; Oppenheim, *Letters*, No. 89.

127. N. de G. Davies, *The Rock Tombs of El-Amarna* (6 vols.; London: Egypt Exploration Fund, 1903–1908), cited by Barucq, *L'expression*, p. 209.

Of all the lands of varied speech,
You know their plans, you scan their way.
The whole of mankind bows to you,
Šamaš, the universe longs for your light (Hymn to Šamaš, ll. 49-52).[128]

The righteous especially are under Yahweh's surveillance.[129] The same is, or should be, true of the king: Ibassi-ilu expresses the wish 'May the eyes of the king be upon me' in a letter to Esarhaddon (ABL 498 [SAA 13, No. 174], l. R11; Oppenheim, *Letters*, No. 130); and a poem expressing good wishes to a New Kingdom pharaoh is full of admiration for this aspect of the king's rule:

> You are told the condition of every country while you are at rest in the palace. You hear the speech of all countries, you possess millions of ears. Your eye is more radiant than the stars of heaven, you can see better than the solar disk. If a person speaks, though the utterance be from a cavern, it comes down to your ear. If anything is done that is hidden, yet your eye will see it. (Caminos, *Miscellanies*, p. 49 = 153; Erman, *Ancient Egyptians*, p. 280).

---

128. Lambert, *Babylonian Wisdom Literature*, p. 129; *ANET*, p. 388; *SAHG* B 4; *HPD*, pp. 51-63; *Before the Muses*, III.32, p. 533.
129. Pss. 33.18; 34.15.

9

IMPLICATIONS AND LIMITATIONS

Terminology

This study, in common with most modern studies of the Psalter, has presupposed Gunkel's classification of the psalms into genres.[1] Although it has been noted that psalms in other categories are in the nature of appeals to God,[2] the focus has been mainly on *Die Klagelieder des Volkes* and *Die Klagelieder des Einzelnen*, usually translated 'Communal Laments' and 'Individual Laments'.[3] However, two questions may be asked: Is 'lament' the best translation of *Klage*? and, Is *Klagelied* the best description of the psalms in question? Whereas the English 'lament' is a response to a situation about which nothing can be done, such as the death of Saul and Jonathan (2 Sam. 1.17-27) or the condition of Jerusalem after its fall (Lamentations), the German *Klage* can be used in the sense of a complaint about a situation which can still be rectified. The lament is addressed to no one in particular; the complaint is addressed to someone who may be able to help. Hence some prefer to call the psalms in question 'Communal (or Individual) Complaint Songs'.[4] But hesitations have been expressed about the appropriateness of the term *Klage*. According to Westermann, it is both too broad—covering lament for the dead and lament arising from distress—and too narrow—leaving out other important elements in the psalm.[5] The psalmists understand themselves to be uttering a 'prayer' (תְּפִלָּה) or 'supplication' (תַּחֲנָה, תַּחֲנוּן), in which the actual complaint or description of plight is only one element.[6] According

---

1. Gunkel and Begrich, *Einleitung*.
2. See p. 11 n. 11 above.
3. E.g. Johnson, 'Psalms', pp. 166, 169.
4. E.g. the English translation of Gunkel and Begrich, *Einleitung*; R.C. Culley, *Oral Formulaic Language in the Biblical Psalms* (Near and Middle East Series, 4; Toronto: Toronto University Press, 1967), pp. 99-101; K. Seybold, *Introduction to the Psalms* (Edinburgh: T. & T. Clark, 1990), p. 116; E. Gerstenberger, 'Jeremiah's Complaints', *JBL* 82 (1963), pp. 393-408 (405 n. 50).
5. Westermann, *Praise and Lament*, p. 170 n. 15. Westermann also distinguished between the German *Klage* ('lament') and *Anklage* ('complaint').
6. This is true of the individual psalms. The communal psalms give no indication of how they would be described.

to Gerstenberger, the petition is the heart of the prayer, and 'all the other elements can be interpreted as preparing and supporting the petition'.[7] Hence the type of psalm in question is sometimes termed *Bitte* or *Bittgebet* or 'supplication'.[8]

Although the terms 'communal lament' and 'individual lament' have been retained in this study, it should be seen as supporting the use of a more inclusive term. It is hardly conceivable that anyone would describe the Amarna letters or the Neo-Assyrian letters as 'laments'. They are essentially appeals to the ruler to take action on the writers' behalf, and help to show the psalms in that light.

Who Were the Psalmists?

Unlike the letter writers, the psalmists have been very successful in concealing their identity. They do not give their names, and introduce themselves and their circumstances only in the most general (and often metaphorical) terms. A fairly strong case can be made for regarding the speaker as the king in most if not all of the individual complaints and thanksgivings, whether or not he composed them himself.[9] This is based on the tradition which associates so many of these psalms with David; on the use of expressions such as 'my God' that are taken to indicate a more intimate relationship with God than the ordinary worshipper would experience; and on the fact that the psalmist is represented as having many enemies and being engaged in battle with them. The chief difficulty is the marked difference in style between the unambiguously royal psalms and the individual complaints. But other features of the psalms of the individual have suggested that some at least are the prayers of private persons attempting to clear themselves of unjust accusations,[10] or seeking asylum because their lives are threatened,[11] or resorting to cultic procedures in the course of litigation.[12] The strength of these proposals is that they are related to institutions which are attested elsewhere in the Hebrew Bible; their weakness is that there are no clear references to these

7. E. Gerstenberger, *Psalms, Part I. with an Introduction to Cultic Poetry* (FOTL, 14; Grand Rapids: Eerdmans, 1988), p. 13.

8. W. Beyerlin, *Die Rettung der Bedrängten in den Feindpsalmen der Einzelnen auf institutionelle Zusammenhänge untersucht* (FRLANT, 99; Göttingen: Vandenhoeck & Ruprecht, 1970), p. 153; R. Alter, 'Psalms', in R. Alter and F. Kermode, *The Literary Guide to the Bible* (London: Fontana Press, 1997), pp. 244-62 (247-48).

9. H. Birkeland, *Die Feinde des Individuums in der israelitischen Psalmenliteratur* (Oslo: Grøndahl, 1933); J.H. Eaton, *Kingship and the Psalms* (The Biblical Seminar; Sheffield: JSOT Press, 2nd edn, 1986).

10. Schmidt, *Gebet des Angeklagten.*

11. L. Delekat, *Asylie und Schutzorakel am Zionheiligtum* (Leiden: E.J. Brill, 1967).

12. Beyerlin, *Rettung der Bedrängten.*

institutions (such as asylum or trial by ordeal) in the psalms and that it is not
clear from their description elsewhere why these procedures should require
the composition and recitation of psalms.

The ancient Near Eastern archives have yielded letters by a great number
of people. Some are written by vassal kings to their Hittite or Egyptian overlords; some by the governors of outlying provinces; some by scholars—
priests, diviners or exorcists—at the Assyrian court; some by or on behalf of
the citizens of a particular city. There is evidence that the letters of kings and
officials were written (and read) by professional scribes, but at the dictation
of the king or official concerned. The overall impression is that there was a
wide circle of people in the ancient Near East over many centuries who were
accustomed to expressing themselves in writing, chiefly in relation to their
needs in their everyday lives.

Although pre-exilic Israel may not have been as advanced culturally as
Egypt and Mesopotamia and estimates of the level of literacy may be prob-
lematic,[13] it is not at all improbable that a similar wide circle of people
communicated by letter when need arose and therefore were accustomed to
expressing themselves in writing as well as orally. Most of the Amarna letters
were written from cities in or near Canaan, and it is unlikely that literacy
skills would have been lost in whatever political or cultural changes took
place subsequently. It was certainly the understanding of Israel's historians
that rulers wrote and received letters (2 Sam. 11.14-15; 1 Kgs 21.8; 2 Kgs
5.5; 10.1; 19.14; 20.12; 2 Chron. 30.1, 6); a prophet might also do so (Jer.
29.1). Then we have the direct epigraphic evidence: the 48 letters which have
been discovered, mainly at Tell ed-Duweir (biblical Lachish) and Arad.

The extant letters are strictly functional and no literary merit can be
claimed for them, though the writer of the Lachish letters replies spiritedly to
accusations of neglect which have apparently been made. Not all those who
could read and write would have thought of composing psalms. But it is at
least a possibility that the psalms were contributed by a similar range of
people in a variety of circumstances. Who those people were and what their
circumstances were we shall never be able to assert with any certainty, but
some suggestions may be made.

The interpretation of the individual psalms as spoken by a king cannot be
easily dismissed, but some of the arguments may not be as strong as at first
appears. The fact that the ancient Near Eastern letter writers routinely address
the king as 'the king my lord' suggests that for the psalmists to address God
as 'my God' is not necessarily an indication of special intimacy, but rather an
expression of loyalty and dependence, and may have come naturally to those
who asserted their loyalty to and dependence upon a human ruler. In some

---

13. D.W. Jamieson-Drake, *Scribes and Schools in Monarchic Judah* (The Social
World of Biblical Antiquity, 9; JSOTSup, 109; Sheffield: Almond Press, 1991).

instances the enemies envisaged are foreign nations (Pss. 9–10; 18) and the circumstances are those of war (Ps. 27). But in others the enemies are closer to hand, neighbours and acquaintances, people who pass the psalmist in the street or call on him (Pss. 31.12 [EVV 11]; 38.12 [EVV 11]; 41.6-7 [EVV 5-6]; 55.10, 12 [EVV 9, 11]; 88.9, 19 [EVV 8, 18]), even former close friends and relatives (Pss. 41.10 [EVV 9]; 55.13-15 [EVV 12-14]; 69.9 [EVV 8]). References to war here (Pss. 55.19, 22 [EVV 18, 21]; 56.2-3 [EVV 1-2]) border on the metaphorical: the element of physical danger is clearly there, but the enemies' chief weapons are the smooth words they speak to the psalmist himself and the slanderous words they speak behind his back (Pss. 55.22 [EVV 21]; 57.5 [EVV 4]; 59.8 [EVV 7]; 64.4 [EVV 3]; 120.3-4). The psalmist could be a king, but there is no compelling reason to assume this. Psalm 59 is particularly ambiguous: the psalmist asks God to 'punish all the nations' (vv. 6, 9 [EVV 5, 8]), but his enemies lie in wait for him and prowl about the city every evening (vv. 4, 7-8 [EVV 3, 6-7]). There is just a hint of anti-monarchical sentiment in Ps. 76.13 [EVV 12]).

Psalm 107 catalogues some of those who would be expected to cry to Yahweh in their distress and to thank him for deliverance: refugees (vv. 4-9), prisoners (vv. 10-16), sick people (vv. 17-22) and sailors (vv. 23-32). Sickness is clearly the reason for the complaint or thanksgiving in Pss. 30; 38; 88; and 116, but in others there are complaints about enemies as well (Pss. 6; 22; 41). The one explicit reference to imprisonment is in Ps. 142.8 (EVV 7). It is possible that some of the psalms in which the psalmist appeals to God for refuge or protection (Pss. 7.2 [EVV 1]; 11.1; 16.1; 31.2 [EVV 1]; 43.2; 71.1; 141.8) are the prayers of asylum seekers in the modern sense rather than those seeking sanctuary from blood vengeance, in the kind of situation envisaged in Isa. 16.3-4; 21.14-15; Obadiah 14 and Ruth 2.12.

The psalmists frequently describe themselves as 'poor and needy' (Pss. 40.18 [EVV 17]; 70.6 [EVV 5]; 86.1; 109.22). This need not mean that they were chronically poor in the economic sense. In other places they pray on behalf of the poor and the oppressed (Pss. 9.19 [EVV 18]; 10.12, 17-18; 12.6 [EVV 5]). The expression may be used in the sense of 'the poor in spirit' (Mt. 5.3). Or they may be temporarily poor, suffering the kind of hardships of which the letter writers complained. Psalm 71 stands out as the prayer of a man experiencing the anxieties that old age brings (vv. 9, 18).

Many of the psalmists regard themselves as members of a group: of the righteous (צַדִּיקִים, Pss. 5.13 [EVV 12]; 64.11 [EVV 10]; 140.14 [EVV 13]), the faithful or loyal (חֲסִידִים, אֱמוּנִים, Pss. 4.4. [EVV 3]; 30.5 [EVV 4]; 31.24 [EVV 23]; 32.6), the humble (עֲנָוִים, Ps 25.9) or the upright (יְשָׁרִים, Pss. 36.11 [EVV 10]; 64.11 [EVV 10]; 140.14 [EVV 13]). These expressions, and the psalmist's self-designation as 'your servant', are further affirmations of loyalty to God.

Hitherto we have assumed that that the experiences described in the individual psalms were those of the psalmists themselves. It has frequently been supposed, however, that the psalms were composed, not by the petitioners themselves, but by professional poets, the guilds of temple singers or cultic prophets. The grounds for this are that the composition of psalms requires skills that the ordinary worshipper would not have; that the formulaic and metaphorical language suggests compositions for repeated use; and that the later use of the psalms and the analogy of modern hymn books attests the willingness of worshippers to use prayers written by others. The temple singers are represented in 1 Chron. 16.4-36 as singing, and presumably composing, psalms, and the name of Asaph, their leader, appears in the superscriptions to Psalms 50 and 73–83. It may be pointed out, however, that the psalms in 1 Chronicles 16—Psalms 106 and 105—are hymns, which would naturally be composed to be sung by or on behalf of a congregation of worshippers, and that none of the Asaphite psalms is a typical individual petition. While it is entirely understandable that people should ask a prophet to intercede for them (1 Sam. 7.8; 12.19, 23; 1 Kgs 17.17-24; Jer. 37.3; 42.2-4), the idea that a prophet or other cultic functionary should pray *in the name of* another person or compose a psalm for that person to sing or recite is much less plausible. It is hard to think of the note of urgency as coming from anything other than the authors' own experience. Perhaps some of the psalmists were prophets or members of the temple personnel and the others were people closely associated with the temple or the court—a fairly restricted circle of literate people of standing, familiar with the traditional formulas and metaphors which are repeatedly drawn upon. The analogy with modern hymn books does not suggest a different conclusion: the authors of many hymns are first of all expressing their own faith and experience, though making it available for others to enter into and use.

The Psalms and the Cult

Many interpreters of the psalms have concluded that the psalms of the individual were sung or spoken or inscribed at a sanctuary, generally the Temple in Jerusalem. The most specific argument is the number of references to 'taking refuge under Yahweh's wings' (Pss. 17.8; 36.8 [EVV 7]; 57.2 [EVV 1]; 61.5 [EVV 4]; 63.8 [EVV 7]; 91.4). These are understood as indicating that the psalmist has literally put himself under God's protection by taking refuge under the wings of the cherubim in the innermost room of the Temple[14] or at

---

14. A.Weiser, *The Psalms* (trans. H. Hartwell; OTL; London: SCM Press, 1962), p. 426; H.-J. Kraus, *Psalms 1–59* (trans. Hilton C. Oswald; Minneapolis: Augsburg Press, 1988), p. 69.

least in their immediate vicinity, in the Temple area.[15] There are, however, difficulties with this interpretation. Literally taking refuge under the wings of the cherubim invites the question: Did the ordinary worshipper have access to the inner sanctuary? It was the understanding of the author of the Epistle to the Hebrews that even the priests did not enter it, except for the high priest, and even he only once a year to make atonement (Heb. 9.6-7). This of course may have been a misunderstanding. The instructions for the making of the altar of incense say that Aaron (= the high priest) had the twice daily duty to offer incense on it (Exod. 30.7-8). And the restriction on access may have been a post-exilic innovation. The Chronicler's account of Uzziah's presumption in offering incense on the altar allows that the priests generally might carry out this duty (2 Chron. 26.16-20), and the story of Korah's revolt suggests that there was a time when any member of the congregation might offer incense (Num. 16). An altar of incense, distinct from the altar on which other sacrifices were offered, may in itself have been an innovation in the Second Temple: there is no mention of such an altar in the account of the building of Solomon's Temple, and earlier sanctuaries would seem to have had a single altar of earth or stone for all purposes (Exod. 20.24-26; Deut. 27.5-8; Josh. 8.30-31). One of those purposes was to provide a place of sanctuary for a person who had committed manslaughter or killed another accidentally (Exod. 21.12-14; cf. Deut. 19.4-5) or was otherwise in fear of his life (1 Kgs 1.50; 2.28). The fugitive grasped the horns of the altar, and therefore, if any of the psalms are to be seen in the context of seeking asylum, it is surprising that there is no mention of the altar and its horns, but only of sheltering under God's wings. A further difficulty is that it is unlikely that the wings of the cherubim would be termed 'God's wings'. The wings of the cherubim enable them to fly and draw the divine chariot (Ps. 18.11 [EVV 10]; Ezek. 1; 10); they have no protective function. On the other hand, Ruth may be said to have taken refuge under the wings of the God of Israel (Ruth 2.12) in a context which is clearly not cultic but indicative of the choice she has made: 'Your people shall be my people, and your God my God' (Ruth 1.16). In Ps. 17.8 'hide me under the shadow of your wings' is balanced by 'guard me like the pupil of the eye'—a highly figurative expression and nothing at all to do with the Temple. As with the references to the king's shadow mentioned above, 'the shadow of God's wings' in the Psalms is a metaphor for God's protection in general without any reference to the contents of the Temple and their supposed function in cases of asylum.

One of the ways of explaining the transition from complaint to confidence in the individual psalms is that the worshipper, present at a festival in Jerusalem, shared in the experience of a 'theophany', 'Yahweh's self-revelation in

15. Beyerlin, *Rettung der Bedrängten*, p. 131.

the presence of his people'.[16] Mowinckel understood this to be 'visibly expressed through the symbols and rites' of the enthronement festival and 'the emotional reactions of the congregation'.[17] For Johnson the orientation of the Temple suggested that God's appearance might have been symbolised at the moment when the early morning sun caught the cloud of incense in the inner sanctuary.[18] Weiser envisaged a visual and auditory experience: the congregation witnessed a 'primitive drama', in which the Sinai event was re-created, God's presence being symbolised by the cloud of incense (Lev. 16.2; 1 Kgs 8.10-11) and the congregation responding by shouting and blowing of trumpets (Ps. 47.6 [EVV 5]).[19] Kraus resisted the idea that the theophany could be produced by a 'manipulation of scenes', and thought that God's appearing would be declared in a 'charismatic proclamation' by a prophet.[20] That there were festivals celebrated in Jerusalem is beyond dispute, though whether one of them was characterised by the enthronement of Yahweh or the renewal of the Sinai covenant or the reaffirmation of the election of Zion may still be debated. That individuals claimed to have seen God in the Temple is also beyond dispute (Isa. 6; Ps. 63.3 [EVV 2]). However, it is not at all certain that such individual experiences were the result of witnessing a ritual drama in the Temple at a festival: one prophet claimed to have seen God elsewhere, when no festival was taking place (Ezek. 1; 10.20); another seems to have received his vision after being summoned by the king to 'inquire' of God (1 Kgs 22.7-23). It is also unlikely that a psalmist in dire straits would have been reassured by a general reaffirmation of God's concern for Israel. The analogy of the letters strongly suggests that only intervention in his own case, or at the very least an assurance of swift intervention, would have satisfied him. We have also seen that the language of 'seeing' the king is more impor-tant for its connotation of receiving the king's attention than for its literal reference. The psalmist is more anxious to be heard than to have or share in

16. Weiser, *Psalms*, p. 29.

17. Mowinckel, *Psalms*, I, p. 142.

18. A.R. Johnson, 'The Role of the King in the Jerusalem Cultus', in S.H. Hooke (ed.), *The Labyrinth: Further Studies in the Relation between Myth and Ritual in the Ancient World* (London: SPCK, 1935), pp. 71-111 (83, 97, 111), referring to F.J. Hollis, 'The Sun-Cult and the Temple at Jerusalem', in S.H. Hooke (ed.), *Myth and Ritual: Essays on the Myth and Ritual of the Hebrews in Relation to the Culture Pattern of the Ancient East* (London: Oxford University Press, 1933), pp. 87-110 (104).

19. A. Weiser, 'Zur Frage nach den Beziehungen der Psalmen zum Kult: Die Darstel-lung der Theophanie in den Psalmen und im Festkult', in W. Baumgartner, O. Eissfeldt, K. Elliger and L. Rost (eds.), *Festschrift für Alfred Bertholet* (Tübingen: J.C.B. Mohr, 1950), pp. 513-31 (523); reprinted in *idem, Glaube und Geschichte im Alten Testament* (Göttingen: Vandenhoeck & Ruprecht, 1961), pp. 303-21 (313); *idem, Psalms*, pp. 29-30, 488 n. 1.

20. Kraus, *Psalms 1–59*, pp. 70-71.

a visual experience (Pss. 4.2 [EVV 1]; 5.2-4 [EVV 1-3]; 17.1-2, 6; 28.1-2; 31.3 [EVV 2]; 39.13 [EVV 12]; 54.4 [EVV 2]; 55.2 [EVV 1]; 61.2 [EVV 1]; 64.2 [EVV 1]; 86.1; 88.3 [EVV 2]; 102.2-3 [EVV 1-2]).

The Collections of the Psalms

It has long been recognised that the Psalter must have been compiled from earlier collections, and Michael Goulder in a number of studies has argued that these collections and the order of the psalms within them are the key to the interpretation of the particular psalms. They were used in parallel with various narrative histories in liturgies performed at different periods and at different sanctuaries. The study most relevant to our present concerns is that on Psalms 51–72,[21] since it contains many of the individual complaints. Goulder points out that these psalms exhibit 'a web of common language and ideas' (though this is illustrated from only nine of the twenty-two psalms) and maintains that 'the only plausible motive for the collection is liturgical'. The psalms are related to the incidents of the Succession Narrative with great ingenuity ('far too interesting to be acceptable') and the interpretation of some details undoubtedly benefits from this fresh approach. But it is difficult to accept that psalms as different in character as 53 (virtually the same psalm as 14), 60 (which shares a passage with 108), 68 and 72 were composed for the same liturgical sequence, and the nine psalms which exhibit 'common language and ideas' have more in common with individual complaints outside the collection than with many of the psalms within it. Our study of the themes and motifs which appear in both the psalms and the ancient Near Eastern letters points to a general outlook and habits of thought rather than to a specific liturgical context.

Structure and Arrangement

Some recent study of the psalms has focussed on the structure of individual psalms and on signs that their present arrangement is deliberate rather than haphazard.[22] It is hardly necessary to say that this study has nothing to contribute along these lines. The emphasis here has been on the themes and

21. M. Goulder, *The Prayers of David (Psalms 51–72)* (Studies in the Psalter, 2; JSOTSup, 102; Sheffield: JSOT Press, 1990).

22. Notably P. Auffret, *La sagesse a bâti sa maison: Études de structures littéraires dans l'Ancien Testament et spécialement dans les Psaumes* (OBO, 49; Freiburg: Éditions Universitaires; Göttingen: Vandenhoeck & Ruprecht, 1982), and many other publications; G.H. Wilson, *The Editing of the Hebrew Psalter* (SBLDS, 76; Chico, CA: Scholars Press, 1985); J.C. McCann (ed.), *The Shape and Shaping of the Psalter* (JSOTSup, 159; Sheffield: Sheffield Academic Press, 1993).

motifs that recur, irrespective of the structure of the psalms or of their position in the Psalter. R.C. Culley, in his study of formulaic expressions and
their distribution in the Psalter, suggested that themes or motifs, 'elements of
subject matter or a group of ideas repeated in a variable form', might usefully
be investigated as 'an intermediate structural device between the line and the
poem itself'.[23] This would of course demand an examination of complete
psalms to discover how the themes or motifs that have been identified interact
and contribute to the impact of the psalm.

Thematic Analysis

The kind of analysis to which this study might lead would differ from the
form-critical analysis which identifies the structural elements in a psalm
(invocation, lament, confession of trust, petition, vow of praise),[24] and from
the stylistic analysis which uncovers the artistic devices employed (inclusio,
chiasmus, repetition, word-play, alliteration, assonance).[25] It would not be
chiefly concerned to identify the cultic background. It would assume that the
intention of the psalm is to persuade God to intervene on behalf of the
individual or the people, and to show how the arguments stated or implied
contribute to that end. We can only offer a few examples here. Psalms 25–28
form a convenient group of the psalms of petition under consideration, similar in intent but varied in expression.

Psalm 25
Psalm 25 relies heavily on expressions of dependence. The psalmist trusts
God (v. 2), waits patiently for him (vv. 3, 5, 21), fixes his gaze upon him
(v. 15), and takes refuge in him (v. 20). He pleads for forgiveness (vv. 7, 11,
18). The appeal to God's character, his mercy, loyalty (חֶסֶד) and faithfulness
(vv. 6, 7, 10), exhibited in his past deeds (v. 6), may be read straightfor-
wardly as a ground of confidence, or possibly as a gentle reproach: Why are
these attributes not in evidence in my life? There is also an understated
appeal to God's own interests: if believers are put to shame (vv. 2, 3, 20), by
suffering ill fortune and becoming objects of scorn, it is God's reputation for
mercy and loyalty that will suffer. The psalmist of course recognises that
expecting God to keep his covenant obligations demands a corresponding

---

23. Culley, *Oral Formulaic Language*, pp. 99-100.

24. E.g Westermann, *Praise and Lament*, pp. 52, 64, 170. Cf. Gunkel and Begrich,
Einleitung; Gerstenberger, *Psalms, Part 1*, and *idem*, *Psalms, Part 2, and Lamentations*
(FOTL, 15; Grand Rapids: Eerdmans, 2001).

25. E.g. N.H. Ridderbos, *Die Psalmen: Stilistische Verfahren und Aufbau mit besonderer Berücksichtigung von Ps 1–41* (BZAW, 117; Berlin: W. de Gruyter, 1972); Auffret,
La Sagesse, etc.

readiness on the part of the human partners in the covenant to do what God expects of them (v. 10). They must display integrity and uprightness (v. 21) and to that end rely on God's guidance and instruction (vv. 4, 5, 8, 9, 14).

The psalm does not stand out, however, as a passionate plea for God's intervention. The acrostic form of course imposes constraints. But there does not seem to be any urgency about the petition. The references to the psalmist's enemies are few, brief and widely separated (vv. 2, 3, 19). Although the appeal at the beginning and the end is addressed to God (vv. 1-7, 16-22), the middle of the psalm has a different audience in mind: those who need to realise afresh the goodness of God and the rewards of living in the right way (vv. 8-10, 12-15). The claim that this is deliberate artistry is questionable, as one of the appeals for pardon comes in the middle of the didactic section (v. 11). The psalmist is lonely and afflicted (v. 16), but his distress is only briefly alluded to, and then in the most general terms. Despite the deployment of so many of the motivations for God to act, it has to be admitted that none are developed at any length, and that the psalm reads more like an exercise than an outpouring of a person in desperate straits.

Psalm 26

Psalm 26 is dominated by the psalmist's protestation of innocence, not of any specific misdeed, but of following a way of life of which God would disapprove (vv. 1-5). His concept of the virtuous life is similar to that expressed in Psalm 1: he shuns the company of the wicked (vv. 4, 9-10). He symbolises his blameless life by a ritual act of handwashing (v. 6). He promises to testify publicly to God's goodness (vv. 7, 12) and professes his love for God's house (v. 8). Nevertheless he fears that despite his good character and unfailing trust (v. 1) he will not be treated any better than violent and corrupt men (vv. 9-10). This ought not to happen; the righteous should prosper (cf. Pss. 1.1-3; 25.13). Hence his prayer that God will vindicate him (v. 1), redeem him and be gracious to him (v. 11). The protestation of innocence and profession of devotion may be seen as arguments for God to show his favour, and the desired outcome to be a general improvement in the psalmist's fortunes rather than a not guilty verdict on a specific charge.

Psalm 27

Psalm 27, like Psalms 9–10, 40 and 89, begins with confidence (vv. 1-6) but switches to complaint and appeal (vv. 7-14). There is no need to suppose that two psalms of different type have been inappropriately joined together. Although it is only in v. 12 that that the psalmist prays, 'Do not hand me over to my adversaries', the threat is there from the beginning and alluded to at various points (vv. 2-3, 6, 11). If he is not afraid, it is not because there is no danger, but because he can rely on God's protection (v. 5), provision (v. 13) and patronage (v. 10). God's protection is described in metaphorical terms: the desire to be constantly in God's house, offering worship and seeking guidance (vv. 6, 8), is an expression of the psalmist's loyalty rather than an indication that he has taken up permanent asylum in the temple. Another expression of his dependence on God is his willingness to wait patiently for the removal of the danger (v. 14).

Psalm 28

The author of Psalm 28, like that of Psalm 26, is afraid that his fate will be no different from that of the wicked (vv. 1, 3; cf. Ps. 26.9). He does not however complain directly of any ill-treatment he is receiving at their hand. Nor does he appeal to God for help on the ground of his own good character. Avowal of dependence on God's protection comes both at the beginning ('my rock', v. 1) and in the thanksgiving at the end, when he acknowledges that he has been heard. ('Yahweh is my strength and shield, in him my heart trusts... Yahweh is the strength of his people; he is the saving refuge of his anointed', vv. 7, 8). Since mention of any specific distress is lacking, it is doubtful whether the psalmist's gratitude is due to any marked change in his fortunes. He may have received a reassuring oracle, or he may have reached an inner conviction that his prayer has been heard.

Analysis along these lines, with an awareness of the motivations of the ancient Near Eastern letter writers, shows that the individual complaint psalms display considerable variety in the situations envisaged and the arguments deployed. At the same time they illustrate in their different ways how the human situation of petition to a ruler helps to illuminate that of prayer to God.

Theological Significance

Brueggemann has proposed that a helpful way to understand the 'function' of the psalms is as a sequence of orientation–disorientation–reorientation.[26] This leads to form-critical analysis of the lament or complaint psalms and discussion of their theological significance.[27] Brueggemann argues that the psalmists' situations should be studied from psychological and sociological

26. W. Brueggemann, 'Psalms and the Life of Faith: A Suggested Typology of Function', *JSOT* 17 (1980), pp. 3-32; reprinted in *idem*, *The Psalms and the Life of Faith* (ed. P.D. Miller; Minneapolis: Fortress Press, 1995), pp. 3-32; *idem*, *The Message of the Psalms: A Theological Commentary* (Augsburg Old Testament Studies; Minneapolis: Augsburg Press, 1984).

27. W. Brueggemann, 'From Hurt to Joy, from Death to Life', *Int* 28 (1974), pp. 3-19; reprinted in *Psalms and the Life of Faith*, pp. 67-83; *idem*, 'The Costly Loss of Lament', *JSOT* 36 (1986), pp. 57-71; reprinted in *Psalms and the Life of Faith*, pp. 98-111.

standpoints as well as purely religious ones. The analogy of the letters certainly supports the attempt to understand 'the political, economic and social' aspects of the complaint. Less convincing is the claim that the reorientation represented by the thanksgiving psalms and the thanksgiving element in the complaint psalms is radically different from the previous orientation. Restoration of the *status quo ante* is what most of the psalmists and letter writers hope for. Anything beyond that is expressed very tentatively.[28]

Study of the Letters

This study has been greatly facilitated by the excellent editions and translations of the various collections of ancient Near Eastern letters now available. In some ways they have been better served than the religious literature, which tends to be anthologised rather than treated comprehensively. Careful attention has been given to textual and philological matters, and much effort has been put into establishing the historical and sociological context of the letters and their writers. The work done on the prosopography of the Neo-Assyrian Empire,[29] based to a large extent on the letters, must be the envy of the historians of other civilisations and periods. But commentary on the letters has tended to be restricted to textual and philological matters. The publication of serviceable editions would probably not have been achieved without such self-discipline. It is hoped that this study will stimulate further attempts to explore the way the letter writers thought and conducted their relations with their rulers.

---

28. R. Tomes, 'The Psalms', in S. Bigger (ed.), *Creating the Old Testament: The Emergence of the Hebrew Bible* (Oxford: Basil Blackwell, 1989), pp. 251-67 (264-67).

29. K. Radner *et al.* (eds.), *The Prosopography of the Neo-Assyrian Empire I.1: A; I.2: B-G; II.2: L-N; III.1: P-S* (Helsinki: Neo-Assyrian Text Corpus Project, 1998–).

APPENDIX

THE AMARNA LETTERS AND CANAANITE HYMNS

It was noted above that the Amarna letters contain passages whose language and metrical structure are reminiscent of passages in the Hebrew psalms,[1] and that some scholars suggested that these were extracts from hymns to a Canaanite god, and only secondarily applied to the pharaoh to whom the letters were written.[2] The Amarna letters would thus be indirect evidence for some of the content of Canaanite hymnody. Here we shall examine this thesis in greater detail than would have been appropriate in the main text.

If we take as an example EA 264, ll. 15-19,

> Should we go up into the sky: *ša-me-ma*, or should we go down into the netherworld, our head: *ru-šu-nu*, is in your hand,

the argument runs as follows. The passage occurs in the middle of a report on quite mundane matters. Tagi of Gezer is apologising that a promised caravan has not been sent to Egypt. The change to an elevated style suggests a quotation. Two words—'sky' and 'our head'—are accompanied by Canaanite glosses. This suggests that the source of the quotation is not Akkadian but Canaanite. The passage can also easily be translated into Hebrew verse. The original is thus likely to be a poem of some kind. And the striking resemblance of the content to that of an actual Hebrew psalm (Ps. 139.8-9) suggests that the quotation was being made from a religious hymn.

The argument is at its strongest in relation to this particular passage. No other passage shows all the features mentioned quite so clearly. However, the argument for quotation is supported by the fact that other passages almost

---

1. O. Weber, in Knudtzon, *Die El-Amarna Tafeln*, II, pp. 1128, 1153, 1195-96, 1229, 1243, 1281, 1323-24.

2. F.H.Th. Böhl, 'Hymnisches und rhythmisches in den Amarnabriefen aus Kanaan', *Theologisches Literaturblatt* 35 (1914), cols. 337-40; reprinted in *Opera minora* (Gröningen/Jakarta: J.B. Wolters, 1953), pp. 375-79; A. Jirku, *Altorientalische Kommentar zum Alten Testament* (Leipzig: A. Deichert, 1923), pp. 220-33; *idem*, 'Kanaanische Psalmenfragmente in der vorisraelitischen Zeit Palästinas und Syriens', *JBL* 52 (1933), pp. 108-20; reprinted in *Von Jerusalem nach Ugarit* (Graz: Akademische Druck- und Verlagsanstalt, 1966), pp. 331-44; Widengren, *Psalms of Lamentation*, p. 5.

identical in wording—EA 292, ll. 8-17; 296, ll. 11-22; and 266, ll. 9-25—occur in letters by different writers. How could they coincide if they were not all quoting from a common source?

Strong as the case may appear to be at first sight, it has to meet five objections:

(1) It has not been confirmed from the Ras Shamra texts. The Amarna letters were of course discovered in 1887; Knudtzon's edition of them was completed in 1915; and Böhl and Jirku had both put forward the theory of quotation from Canaanite hymns before 1928, when the first discoveries were made at Ras Shamra. They must have been disappointed that none but the merest fragments of Canaanite hymns have been discovered[3] and that the mythological texts have not yielded any striking parallels to the Amarna passages in a religious context. Even if we turn to Psalm 29, the Hebrew psalm which is thought to be most probably an adaptation of a Canaanite psalm, because of its parallels with Ugaritic texts, the affinities with these Amarna passages are slight. In the psalm 'the God of glory thunders'; in EA 147, ll. 9-15 the pharaoh 'thunders in the sky like Baal so that the whole land trembles at his thunder'. In the psalm Yahweh 'will bless his people with peace'; in EA the pharaoh 'establishes the whole land in peace by the power of his arm'. It is true that one is more likely to say that a god thunders than that a king thunders, and so the latter idea must be secondary to the former. But the source need not be Canaanite hymnody, as we shall see. It is more immediately obvious that the king has established the land in peace than that God has; there is no good reason therefore for assuming that this was originally a religious idea. In the psalm the line comes in the context of Yahweh's enthronement as king, so that it may be a conscious elaboration of that analogy. But even if the parallels were more significant than they are, we should still not be sure that the psalm was originally Canaanite. Direct confirmation from Canaan of the Böhl–Jirku thesis would still be lacking.

(2) The motifs which are common to the Amarna letters and to known hymns and psalms are not confined to these 'poetic' passages. Böhl and Jirku concentrated on what we have termed 'expressions of dependence' which are common to the Amarna letters and to psalms and hymns, such as the mighty hand or arm of the king, his life-giving breath, his protection rising like a wall of bronze, his being father and lord to his servant, seeking his face. But both letter writer and psalmist protest their loyalty. When Lab'ayu says,

> The fact is that I am a loyal servant of the king! I am not a rebel and I am not delinquent in duty. I have not held back my payments of tribute; I have not held back anything requested by my commissioner (EA 264, ll.10-15),

---

3. RS 94, 95 (Akkadian); RS 13 + 43 (Ugaritic); see Mowinckel, 'Psalm Criticism', pp. 14-15; *Psalms*, II, p. 187.

he is really doing the same as the psalmist when he says

> I have followed the ways of Yahweh
> and have not turned wickedly from my God;
> all his laws are before my eyes,
> I have not failed to follow his decrees (Ps. 18.21-22).

Both are protesting their loyalty. Neither is quoting from the other, but it is natural for the psalmist to approach God in the same way as he would approach the king. Similarly, when 'Abdi-Heba says,

> As the king has placed his name in Jerusalem for ever, he cannot abandon it
> (EA 287, ll. 60-63),

he is appealing to the king's own interests in the same way as the psalmist appeals to God's:

> Remember the assembly of your people
> taken long since for your own,
> and Mount Zion, which was your home (Ps. 74.2).

The analogies between the Amarna letters and religious literature are thus much wider than Böhl or Jirku recognised, and the expressions of dependence which attracted their attention need to be considered as one set of motifs among a number.

(3) High flown language in letters is not confined to the Amarna texts. The Assyrian exorcist Adad-šumu-usur could be most eloquent and original in his praise of the king.[4] Something must be allowed to the skill and imagination of the letter writers. Furthermore, the standard opening of an Amarna letter—

> At the feet of my lord, my sun,
> seven times and seven times I fall down—

is very similar to that of Akkadian letters at Ugarit—

> At the feet of my master, from afar,
> twice seven times I fall down.

Some of the features of Akkadian political correspondence are thus international, and it should not be assumed too readily that any elements in it have a purely local origin.

(4) There have been one or two attempts to show that some of the motifs in question can be found used of the king in Egyptian inscriptions. Alt drew attention to four examples in an article published in 1933[5] and Albright

---

4. See, e.g., Oppenheim, *Letters*, Nos. 86; 87; 96.
5. A. Alt, 'Hic murus aheneus esto', *ZDMG* 86 (1933), pp. 33-48.

argued in 1937 for the Egyptian background of the ideas, idioms and word order of EA 147, ll. 5-15 and 41-56.[6] Further evidence can also be supplied.

(a) Alt's first example was the comparison of the pharaoh with Baal in EA 147, ll. 10-15,

who thunders in the sky like Baal so that the whole land trembles at the sound.[7]

This sounds like clear evidence of a Canaanite source, until we realise that a number of Asiatic gods were domesticated in Egypt, and that Baal is the one most frequently mentioned.[8] Baal was equated with the Egyptian war gods, Montu and Seth, and his name was used in figures of speech relating to the pharaoh's prowess in battle. The comparison is very frequent in the records of Ramesses III ('He appears on the battlefield like Baal', 'He is like Baal at the time of his raging', 'His battle cry is like (that of) Baal in the heavens'),[9] but it also comes earlier, in a papyrus text of the poem on the battle Ramesses II fought at Kadesh.[10] There may be even earlier instances.[11] This use of the name of Baal is possibly a legacy of the Hyksos period in Egypt (eighteenth–sixteenth centuries BCE). In the story of King Apophis and Seqnen-Re we are told that Apophis 'made Seth his lord and served no other god in the whole land beside Seth';[12] and Siegfried Morenz comments: 'Here it may be assumed that Seth stands for the Syrian god Baal, because of all foreign deities Baal alone is designated in later Egyptian texts by Seth's animal'.[13] Thus the comparison of the pharaoh with Baal could already have been familiar in Egypt by the beginning of the fourteenth century.

(b) In EA 147, ll. 41-56, the pharaoh is described as a wall of bronze, and Alt pointed out that Seti I is referred to in that way: 'A great wall of bronze protecting his army'.[14] Ramesses II is described as a 'wall of iron (or

---

6. W.F. Albright, 'The Egyptian Correspondence of Abimilki, Prince of Tyre', *JEA* 23 (1937), pp. 190-203.

7. H. Gressmann argued that the name of the deity should be rendered 'Baal' and not 'Adad': 'Hadad und Baal nach den Amaranabriefen und nach ägyptischen Texte', in W. Frankenberg and F. Kuechler (eds.), *Abhandlungen zur semitischen Religionskunde und sprachwissenschaft* (Festschrift W.W. Graf von Baudissin; BZAW, 33; Giessen: Alfred Töpelmann, 1918), pp. 191-216.

8. J.A. Wilson, in *ANET*, p. 249b.

9. Edgerton and Wilson, *Historical Records of Ramses III*, pp. 9, 60, 94.

10. Pap. Sallier III.3.8-9; J.A. Wilson, in *ANET*, p. 249 n. 10; Davies, *Inscriptions*, pp. 62-63, 68-69, 74-75, 80-81.

11. Seti I: Davies, *Inscriptions*, pp. 2-3, 14-15, 20-21; Gressmann, 'Hadad und Baal', p. 203; Alt, 'Hic murus', p. 38; Albright, 'Abimilki', p. 198.

12. Pap. Sallier I.1-3; Erman, *The Ancient Egyptians*, p. 166; *ANET*, p. 231.

13. S. Morenz, *Egyptian Religion* (trans. Ann E. Keep; London: Methuen, 1960), p. 238.

14. *ARE* III, §224; Davies, *Inscriptions*, pp. 36-37.

"flint")'.[15] Similar expressions are used of the gods Horus and Amun,[16] but instances are too few to suggest that what was originally a religious expression has been adopted as part of the courtly style. The king's protection of his army is constantly emphasised in Egyptian inscriptions, and the comparison of the pharaoh with a wall is older than the Amarna letters. Amenophis II is 'a wall protecting Egypt';[17] Sesostris III is 'a dam and a rampart'.[18]

(c) References to the king's life-giving breath (EA 100, ll. 36-38; 137, ll. 5-15, 41-56) are also frequent in the inscriptions. It is the standard formula for captives pleading for the lives to be spared. 'Give to us the breath, for it is yours, and no one can live without you', say Libyan captives to Ramesses III.[19] 'I am a sovereign beneficent to the trusting, mild, and giving breath to every nostril', says Ramesses III to his princes, officials and commanders.[20] The idiom appears from the time of Thutmose III onwards.[21]

(d) Alt thought that the direct comparison of the Egyptian king with the sun or the sun god (EA 147, ll. 5-15, 41-56[22]) was originally non-Egyptian. The familiar Egyptian title for the king is 'son of Re'; the assumption of the direct title 'the sun' or 'the sun god' is more characteristic of, say, the Hittite kings.[23] However, the direct comparison has a long history in Egypt: the Instruction of Sheetep-ib-Re calls the Twelfth Dynasty King Amenemhet III 'Re, by whose beams one sees'.[24] In the opinion of Morenz the Egyptian king was originally identified with the god, but later people became increasingly aware that he was indeed a human being, and so the term 'son of Re', conveying the notion of 'only just' divine, was added to the titulary from the Fourth Dynasty onwards, alongside 'Horus', the older term expressing identity.[25] EA 147 does not contain any dogmatic identification of the king with Re. Re is clearly the king's father (l. 8), and in l. 52 the reference to the sun is metaphorical, as is that to the wall of bronze. The king's granting of life and protection is analogous to the functions of the sun and the wall. Comparison of the king with the sun or the sun god is frequent in the inscriptions of Amenophis III and Akhenaten.[26] There is no need to postulate any usage but Egyptian behind the references in the Amarna letters.

15.   *ARE* III, §340.; Davies, *Inscriptions*, pp. 120-21.
16.   Alt, 'Hic murus', pp. 40-41.
17.   *ARE* II, §792; Cumming, *Historical Records*, I, p. 26, §1290.
18.   Simpson, *Literature*, p. 282; Lichtheim, *Literature*, I, pp. 199-200.
19.   Edgerton and Wilson, *Ramses III*, p. 71.
20.   Edgerton and Wilson, *Ramses III*, p. 86.
21.   *ARE* II, §257; cf. Davies, *Inscriptions*, pp. 6-7.
22.   Cf. EA 195, ll. 16-23.
23.   Widengren thought that the identification was originally Old Babylonian (*Psalms of Lamentation*, pp. 10-11). Hammurabi is described as 'the sun of Babylon' (CH V, ll. 3-5).
24.   *ANET*, p. 431a; Erman, *Ancient Egyptians*, p. 84.
25.   Morenz, *Egyptian Religion*, pp. 34-36.
26.   *ARE*, II, §§900, 917, 960, 991, 1000.

(e) In his comments on EA 147 Albright maintained that the idea of the sun, or the king as sun, 'giving life by his sweet breath', while well known from Egyptian inscriptions, was unknown in Akkadian; that the phrase 'according to the determination of the sun' represents a familiar Egyptian phrase, and that the idiom translated 'day by day' is unknown in Akkadian, possible in Canaanite, but a more direct equivalent of the Egyptian idiom. Several of the ideas in EA 147, ll. 41-56, are found in a hymn to Amun of the next generation.[27]

> O Amun, you brazen rampart (?)...
> The sun of the one who does not know you, O Amun, sets.
> As for the one who knows you, he rises...
> The whole earth is in light.
> He who puts you entirely into his heart, O Amun,
> Behold, his sun rises.

Language previously used of the king is here used exclusively of the god. Did its author derive it from previous hymns to the god or has he in reaction against exaggerated claims for the king deliberately taken the courtly language of the Amarna age and appropriated it for the god alone?

(f) In EA 73, ll. 35-38, Rib-Hadda says of Amanappa 'You are father and lord to me', and Jirku cited this because 'father' is commonly used to describe the deity in the Hebrew Bible. We may add that this usage is not confined to the Hebrew Bible. Non-Israelite hymns compare the god with father and mother.[28] But Rib-Hadda may be acknowledging Amanappa as his patron, just as in EA 286, ll. 9-13, 287, ll. 25-28 and 288, ll. 13-15, 'Abdi-Heba of Jerusalem is acknowledging the king as his patron. This was not mere rhetoric in the time of the Eighteenth Dynasty. According to W.C. Hayes 'more than one official of the Eighteenth Dynasty boasted that at the start of his career he was "without (influential) kindred" or that he was "humble of family, one of small account in his town"'.[29] The pharaoh's officials were a 'new aristocracy', and it was natural to them to express appreciation of patronage. André Barucq cited evidence[30] that the courtiers of Akhenaten were particularly prone to these sentiments, and maintained that they did borrow the language of religious hymns. One refers to Akhenaten as the one who 'has built me, created me, caused me to exist'; another says that Akhenaten has caused him to take his place 'among men'. The king is the 'destiny of their life', 'breath for every nose that breathes', 'the god who gives life'. The language here is fulsome and no doubt borrowed from religious sources. But the references to

---

27. Cf. Erman, *Ancient Egyptians*, pp. 309-10.

28. E.g. *ANET*, pp. 385-86, 392, 397, 401; *Before the Muses*, I, p. 159, II, pp. 576, 585-87, 589, 672.

29. Hayes, 'Egypt', p. 353.

30. Barucq, *L'expression*, p. 248.

patronage in the Amarna letters are meant quite literally, and are not borrowed from any known hymn.

(g) In EA 147, ll. 5-15, the king 'establishes the entire land in peace, by the power of his arm'. Praise of the king for bringing peaceful conditions is of course one of the themes of the Merenptah stele[31] and it occurs in other inscriptions as well.[32]

(h) The expression 'under the feet of the king' (EA 292, ll. 13-17; 296, ll. 17-22; 266, ll. 16-25) is a very frequent one in Egyptian inscriptions.[33] It expresses subjection, and while it is not an exclusively Egyptian idiom, it is one that is entirely expected in Egyptian documents.

(5) The final objection to the view that the pharaoh's correspondents drew upon Canaanite hymnody is that some of the motifs are to be found in letters *from* the pharaoh. It is not of course sufficient to demonstrate that the motifs are Egyptian: one must also show how the correspondents in Syria and Palestine came across them. Alt believed that there must have existed 'a collection of approved formulas' in Akkadian which correspondents could draw upon when they wrote to the court.[34] This was rejected by Böhl[35] on the ground that there is no trace of such collections in the ancient Near East. We have already seen that the opening formula, 'At the (two) feet of my lord, my sun, seven times and seven times I fall down', must have been common to the Akkadian international correspondence of the time. That there should be formulas for conventional openings to letters and routine reports is understandable enough. It is less likely that there were formulas to cover every variation of content. One source from which correspondents would be likely to learn acceptable expressions, however, would be the pharaoh's own letters. We do not have any matching pair of letters in the Amarna corpus, but we have some ten letters from the king to various vassals, officials and foreign kings. The phrase 'under the two feet of the king', which we have just been considering, occurs in a latter from Amenophis III to Milkilu of Gezer:

> Amun has indeed put the Upper Land, the Lower Land, where the sun, *šamaš*, rises, where the sun, *šamaš*, sets, under the feet of the king (EA 369, ll. 28-32).

We note here that the *king* uses Canaanite glosses in his letters. This shows that, whatever the purpose of the glosses may be, they provide no conclusive evidence that a correspondent is quoting from a Canaanite source. The theory that writers quoted back to the king language he had used in letters to them may possibly explain the occurrence of the same passage in the three letters

---

31. *ANET*, p. 377b; *DOTT*, p. 139.
32. E.g. of Kheti I (*ARE*, I, §404).
33. *ANET*, pp. 199a, 245a, 251a, 257a, 263b.
34. Alt, 'Hic murus', p. 36.
35. Böhl, *Opera Minora*, p. 517.

by different writers. We should have to assume that the king wrote in such terms as these:

> You have looked here and you have looked there, but there is no light. And you have looked upon the king, your lord, and it is bright. And though one brick should move from under another, you shall not move from under the two feet of the king, your lord.

This is not an entirely satisfactory explanation of the coincidence of the three passages. One would expect the writers repeating the king's words to preface them with a formula of quotation, such as, 'You have said...' Another suggestion is that the writers were quoting poems addressed to the king rather than hymns addressed to a god.[36] But it is more likely that something the pharaoh did or said prompted them to write in the same terms than that they each independently quoted from the same hymn or poem or chose the same passage from a stock collection of approved formulas.

A number of the letters mention seeing or seeking the king's face (EA 147, ll. 59-60; 165, ll. 4-8; 166; ll. 6-8; 169, ll. 7-10) or speak of the king giving life (EA 169, ll. 7-10; 238, ll. 29-33). For a possible source for these letters we need look no further than a letter from the pharaoh to Aziru, the ruler of Amurru:

> Come yourself, or send your son, and you will see the king, at whose sight all lands live (EA 162, ll. 48-50).

The description of the king as the sun or as like the sun (EA 147, ll. 5-8, 52-56) was certainly used by the king as well as by his subjects:

> And know that the king is hale like the sun in the sky (EA 162, ll. 78-79; 367, l. 22).

The case for quotation from Canaanite hymns in the Amarna letters is thus a good deal weaker than appeared at first sight. The surmise has not been borne out by any material from Ras Shamra; the motifs which appear in the 'hymnic' passages are familiar from Egyptian sources; some of them even appear in what examples we have of the king's letters. What does emerge from a comparative study of the Amarna letters and religious texts is not that the one contains quotations from the other but that there is a broadly based analogy between the way a man addressed his king and the way he addressed his god, and that for the most part it is the human situation which has imposed its pattern on the religious situation and not vice versa.

---

36. Gunkel and Begrich, *Einleitung*, §5.23.

BIBLIOGRAPHY

Ackroyd, Peter R., 'Criteria for the Maccabean Dating of Old Testament Literature', *VT* 3 (1952), pp. 113-32.

—*Exile and Restoration* (London: SCM Press, 1968).

Albright, W.F., 'The Amarna Letters from Palestine', in Edwards, Gadd, Hammond and Sollenberger (eds.), *History of the Middle East and the Aegean Region c. 1380–1000 BC* (CAH II.2), pp. 98-116.

—'The Egyptian Correspondence of Abimilki, Prince of Tyre', *JEA* 23 (1937), pp. 190-203.

—'An Unrecognised Amarna Letter from Ugarit', *BASOR* 95 (1944), pp. 30-33.

Alt, Albrecht, 'Hic murus aheneus esto', *ZDMG* 86 (1933), pp. 33-48.

Alter, R., 'Psalms', in Alter and Kermode, *The Literary Guide to the Bible* (London: Fontana Press, 1997), pp. 244-62.

Alter, Robert, and Frank Kermode, *The Literary Guide to the Bible* (London: Fontana Press, 1997).

Ap-Thomas, D.R., 'Some Notes on the Old Testament Attitude to Prayer', *SJT* 9 (1956), pp. 422-29.

Auffret, Pierre, *La sagesse a bâti sa maison: Études de structures littéraires dans l'Ancien Testament et spécialement dans les Psaumes* (OBO, 49; Freiburg: Éditions Universitaires; Göttingen: Vandenhoeck & Ruprecht, 1982).

Barr, James, 'Covenant', in Hastings (ed.), *Dictionary of the Bible*, pp. 183-85.

Barucq, André, *L'expression de la louange divine et de la prière dans la Bible et en Égypte* (Bibliothèque d'étude, 33; Cairo: Institut français d'archéologie orientale, 1962).

Batto, B.F., *Studies on Women at Mari* (Baltimore: The Johns Hopkins University Press, 1974).

Baudissin, W.W. Graf von, '"Gott schauen" in der alttestamentlichen Religion', *ARW* 18 (1915), pp. 173-239.

Baumgartner, W., O. Eissfeldt, K. Elliger and L. Rost (eds.), *Festschrift Alfred Bertholet zum 80. Geburtstag gewidmet* (Tübingen: J.C.B. Mohr [Paul Siebeck], 1950).

Begrich, J., 'Die Vertrauensäusserungen im israelitischen Klagelied des Einzelnen und in seinen babylonischen Gegenstücken', *ZAW* 46 (1928), pp. 221-60; reprinted in *Gesammelte Studien zum Alten Testament* (ed. W. Zimmerli; TBü, 21; Munich: Chr. Kaiser Verlag, 1964), pp. 168-216.

Beyerlin, W., *Die Rettung der Bedrängten in den Feindpsalmen der Einzelnen auf institutionelle Zusammenhänge untersucht* (FRLANT, 99; Göttingen: Vandenhoeck & Ruprecht, 1970).

Bickerman, E., 'Couper une alliance', *Archive d'histoire du droit oriental* 5 (1951), pp. 133-56; reprinted in *idem, Studies in Jewish and Christian History: Part One* (Arbeiten zur Geschichte des aniken Judentums und des Urchristentums, 9; Leiden: E.J. Brill, 1976), pp. 1-32.

Bigger, Stephen (ed.), *Creating the Old Testament: The Emergence of the Hebrew Bible* (Oxford: Basil Blackwell, 1989).

Birkeland, Harris, *Die Feinde des Individuums in der israelitischen Psalmenliteratur* (Oslo: Grøndahl, 1933).

Blackman, A.M., 'The Psalms in the Light of Egyptian Research', in Simpson (ed.), *The Psalmists*, pp. 177-97.

Boer, P.A.H. de, *De Voorbede in het Oude Testament* (Leiden: E.J. Brill, 1943) (= *OTS* 3).

Böhl, F.H.Th., 'Hymnisches und rhythmisches in den Amarnabriefen aus Kanaan', *Theologisches Literaturblatt* 35 (1914), cols. 337-40; reprinted in *Opera minora* (Gröningen/Jakarta: J.B. Wolters, 1953), pp. 375-79.

Böllenrücher, J., *Gebete und Hymnen an Nergal* (Leipzig: J.C. Hinrichs, 1904).

Borger, R., *Die Inschriften Asarhaddons, Königs von Assyrien* (*AfO* Beiheft, 9; Graz: E. Weidner, 1956).

Brueggemann, Walter, 'The Costly Loss of Lament', *JSOT* 36 (1986), pp. 57-71; reprinted in *Psalms and the Life of Faith*, pp. 98-111.

—'From Hurt to Joy, from Death to Life', *Int* 28 (1974), pp. 3-19; reprinted in *Psalms and the Life of Faith*, pp. 67-83.

—*The Message of the Psalms: A Theological Commentary* (Augsburg Old Testament Studies; Minneapolis: Augsburg Press, 1984).

—*The Psalms and the Life of Faith* (ed. P.D. Miller; Minneapolis: Fortress Press, 1995), pp. 3-32.

—'Psalms and the Life of Faith: A Suggested Typology of Function', *JSOT* 17 (1980), pp. 3-32; reprinted in *Psalms and the Life of Faith*, pp. 3-32.

Caminos, R.A., *Late Egyptian Miscellanies* (Brown Egyptological Studies, 1; London: Oxford University Press, 1954).

Campbell, E.F., 'The Amarna Letters and the Amarna Period', *BA* 23 (1960), pp. 2-22; reprinted in Campbell and Freedman (eds.), *The Biblical Archaeologist Reader 3*, pp. 54-75.

—*The Chronology of the Amarna Letters* (Baltimore: The Johns Hopkins University Press, 1964).

Campbell, E.F., and D.N. Freedman (eds.), *The Biblical Archaeologist Reader 3* (Garden City, NY: Doubleday, 1970).

Castellino, G.R., *Le lamentazioni individuali e gli Inni in Babilonia e in Israele* (Turin: Societa Editrice Internationale, 1940).

—'Mesopotamian Parallels to some Passages in the Psalms', in Donner, Hanhart and Smend (eds.), *Beiträge zur Alttestamentlichen Theologie*, pp. 60-68.

Černy, J., *Ancient Egyptian Religion* (London: Hutchinson, 1952; repr., Westport, CT: Greenwood Press, 1979).

Churpin, D., F. Joannès, S. Lackenbacher and B. Lafont, *Archives Épistolaires de Mari*, I/2 (Archives royales de Mari, XXVI; Paris: Editions Recherche sur les Civilisations, 1988).

Clifford, Richard J., *Psalms 1–72* (Abingdon Old Testament Commentaries, 1; Nashville: Abingdon Press, 2002).

Cohen, M.E., *The Canonical Lamentations of Ancient Mesopotamia* (2 vols.; Potomac, MD; Capital Decisions, 1988).

—*Sumerian Hymnology: The* eršemma (HUCA Supplement, 2; Cincinnati: Hebrew Union College, 1981).

Cole, S.W., and P. Machinist, *Letters from Priests to the Kings Esarhaddon and Assurbanipal* (SAA, 13; Helsinki: Helsinki University Press, 1998).

Coppens, J., 'Les parallèles du psautier avec les textes de Ras Shamra-Ougarit', *Mélanges L.Th. Lefort = Le Muséon* 59 (1946), pp. 113-42.

Cross, Frank M., *The Ancient Library of Qumran* (London: Gerald Duckworth, 1958).

Cryer, F.H., *Divination in Ancient Israel and its Near Eastern Environment* (JSOTSup, 142; Sheffield: Sheffield Academic Press, 1994).

Culley, R.C., *Oral Formulaic Language in the Biblical Psalms* (Near and Middle East Series, 4; Toronto: Toronto University Press, 1967).

Cumming, B.G., *Egyptian Historical Records of the Later Eighteenth Dynasty* (3 fascicles; Warminster: Aris & Phillips, 1982–84).

Cumming, C.G., *The Assyrian and Hebrew Hymns of Praise* (Columbia University Oriental Studies, 12; New York: Columbia University Press, 1934).

Cunchillos, J.-L. (ed.), *Textes Ugaritiques*. II. *Correspondance: Introduction, traduction, commentaire* (Paris: Cerf, 1989).

Dalglish, E.R., *Psalm Fifty-One in the Light of Ancient Near Eastern Patternism* (Leiden: E.J. Brill, 1962).

Davies, B.G., *Egyptian Historical Inscriptions of the Nineteenth Dynasty* (Jonsered: Paul Aström, 1997).

Davies, N. de G., *The Rock Tombs of El-Amarna* (6 vols.; London: Egypt Exploration Fund, 1903–1908).

Delekat, L., *Asylie und Schutzorakel am Zionheiligtum* (Leiden: E.J. Brill, 1967).

Deller, K., 'Die Briefe der Adad-šumu-usur', in Röllig (ed.), Lišan mithurti, pp. 45-64.

Dietrich, M., *The Neo-Babylonian Correspondence of Sargon and Sennacherib* (SAA, 17; Helsinki: Helsinki University Press, 2003).

Dhorme, E., 'L'emploi métaphorique des noms des parties du corps en hébreu et en akkadien. III. Le visage', *RB* 30 (1921), pp. 374-99.

Donner, H., R. Hanhart and R. Smend (eds.), *Beiträge zur Alttestamentlichen Theologie* Festschrift W. Zimmerli; Göttingen: Vandenhoeck & Ruprecht, 1977).

Driver, G.R., 'The Psalms in the Light of Babylonian Research', in Simpson (ed.) *The Psalmists*, pp. 109-75.

—'Studies in the Vocabulary of the Old Testament V', *JTS* 34 (1933), pp. 33-44.

Drower, Margaret, 'Ugarit in the Fourteenth and Thirteenth Centuries BC', in Edwards, Gadd, Hammond and Sollenberger (eds.), *History of the Middle East and the Aegean Region c. 1380–1000 BC* (CAH II.2), pp. 130-48.

Durand, J.-M., *Archives Épistolaires de Mari*, I/1 (Archives royales de Mari, 26; Paris: Editions Recherche sur les Civilsations, 1988).

Eaton, J.H., *Kingship and the Psalms* (The Biblical Seminar; Sheffield: JSOT Press, 2nd edn, 1986).

—*The Psalms* (Torch Commentaries; London: SCM Press, 1967).

Ebeling, E., *Die akkadische Gebetsserie 'Handerhebung'* (Deutsche Akademie der Wissenschaften zu Berlin, Institut für Orientforschung, Veröffentlichung, No. 20; Berlin: Akademie-Verlag, 1953).

Edgerton, W.F., and J.A. Wilson, *Historical Records of Ramses III* (Oriental Institute of the University of Chicago: Studies in Ancient Oriental Civilisation, 12; Chicago: University of Chicago Press, 1936).

Edwards, I.E.S., C.J. Gadd, N.G.L. Hammond and E. Sollenberger (eds.), *Cambridge Ancient History II.1: History of the Middle East and the Aegean Region c. 1800–1380 BC; II.2 History of the Middle East and the Aegean Region c 1380–1000 BC* (Cambridge: Cambridge University Press, 3rd edn, 1975).

Eissfeldt, Otto, *The Old Testament: An Introduction* (trans. P.R Ackroyd; Oxford: Basil Blackwell, 1965).

Engnell, Ivan, *Studies in Divine Kingship* (Uppsala: Almqvist & Wiksell, 1st edn, 1943 [2nd edn 1967]).

Erman, Adolf, *The Ancient Egyptians: A Sourcebook of their Writings* (trans. A.M. Blackman; New York: Harper & Row, 1966).

Ferris, P.W., Jr, *The Genre of Communal Lament in the Bible and the Ancient Near East* (Atlanta: Scholars Press, 1992).

Fohrer, G., *Introduction to the Old Testament* (London: SPCK, 1970).

—Review of McCarthy, *Treaty and Covenant*, *ZAW* 76 (1964), p. 236.

Frankenberg, W., and F. Kuechler (eds.), *Abhandlungen zur semitischen Religionskunde und sprachwissenschaft* (Festschrift W.W. Graf von Baudissin; BZAW, 33; Giessen: Alfred Töpelmann, 1918).

Frankfort, Henri, and H.A. Frankfort, J.A. Wilson and T. Jacobsen, *Before Philosophy* (Harmondsworth: Penguin Books, 1949).

Fredriksson, H., *Jahwe als Krieger* (Lund: C.W.K. Gleerup, 1945).

Freedman, D.N., and E.F. Campbell (eds.), *The Biblical Archaeologist Reader 2* (Garden City, NY: Doubleday, 1964).

Gadd, C.J., 'The Second Lamentation for Ur', in Thomas and McHardy (eds.), *Hebrew and Semitic Studies*, pp. 59-71.

Gerstenberger, Ernst, 'Covenant and Commandment', *JBL* 84 (1965), pp. 38-51.

—*Der bittende Mensch: Bittritual und Klagelied des Einzelnen im Alten Testament* (WMANT, 51; Neukirchen–Vluyn: Neukirchener Verlag, 1980).

—'Der Klagende Mensch', in H.W. Wolff (ed.), *Problme biblische Theologies. Gerhard von Rad zum 70. Geburtstag* (Munich: Chr. Kaiser Verlag, 1971), pp. 64-72.

—'Jeremiah's Complaints', *JBL* 82 (1963), pp. 393-408.

—*Psalms, Part I, with an Introduction to Cultic Poetry* (FOTL, 14; Grand Rapids: Eerdmans, 1988).

—*Wesen und Herkunft der 'apodiktischen Rechts'* (WMANT, 20; Neukirchen–Vluyn: Neukirchener Verlag, 1965).

Ginsberg, H.L., 'Ugaritic Studies and the Bible', *BA* 8 (1945), pp. 41-58; reprinted in Freedman and Campbell (eds.), *The Biblical Archaeologist Reader 2*, pp. 34-50.

Goetze, A., *Hattušiliš: der Bericht über seine Thronbesteigung nebst den Paralleltexten*, in F. Sommer (ed.), *Hethitische Texte in Umschrift* (Mitteilungen der Vorderasiatisch-Ägyptischen Gesellschaft 29.3 [1924]; Leipzig: J.C. Hinrichs, 1925).

Golla, E., *Der Vertrag des Hattikönigs Mursil mit den König Sunassura von Kiswadna* (Breslau: Schlesische Volkszeitung, 1920).

Goulder, M.D., *The Prayers of David (Psalms 51–72)* (Studies in the Psalter, 2; JSOTSup, 102; Sheffield: JSOT Press, 1990).

Green, M., 'The Eridu Lament', *JCS* 30 (1978), pp. 127-67.

—'The Uruk Lament', *JAOS* 104 (1984), pp. 252-79.

Gressmann, Hugo, 'Hadad und Baal nach den Amarnabriefen und nach ägyptischen Texte', in Frankenberg and Kuechler (eds.), *Abhandlungen zur semitischen Religionskunde und sprachwissenschaft*, pp. 191-216.

—'The Development of Hebrew Psalmody', in Simpson (ed.), *The Psalmists*, pp. 1-21.

Gunkel, Herman, *Die Psalmen* (HKAT, II/2; Göttingen: Vandenhoeck & Ruprecht, 1926).

Gunkel, Herman, and J. Begrich, *Einleitung in die Psalmen* (Göttingen: Vandenhoeck & Ruprecht, 1933); ET *Introduction to Psalms: The Genres of the Religious Lyrics of Israel* (trans. James D. Nogalski; Mercer Library of Biblical Studies; Macon, GA: Mercer University Press, 1998).

Gurney, O.R., *The Hittites* (Harmondsworth: Penguin Books, 2nd edn, 1954).

Gwaltney, W.C., Jr, 'The Biblical Book of Lamentations in the Context of Near Eastern Lament Literature', in Hallo, Moyer and Perdue (eds.), *Scripture in Context*, II, pp. 191-211.

Hallo, W.W., 'Individual Prayer in Sumerian: The Continuity of a Tradition', in *idem* (ed.), *Essays in Memory of E.A. Speiser*, pp. 71-89.

Hallo, W.W. (ed.), *Essays in Memory of E.A. Speiser* (American Oriental Series, 53; New Haven: American Oriental Society, 1968 [= *JAOS* 88/1]).

Hallo, W.W., J.C. Moyer and L.G. Perdue (eds.), *Scripture in Context. II: More Essays on the Comparative Method* (Winona Lake, IN: Eisenbrauns, 1983).

Hastings, James (ed.), *Dictionary of the Bible* (rev. F.C. Grant and H.H. Rowley; Edinburgh: T. & T. Clark, 2nd edn, 1963).

Hayes, W.C., 'Egypt: Internal Affairs from Tuthmosis I to the Death of Amenophis III', in Edwards, Gadd, Hammond and Sollenberger (eds.), *History of the Middle East and the Aegean Region c. 1800–1380 BC* (CAH II.1), pp. 313-416.

Heiler, Friedrich, *Prayer* (trans. S. McComb; London: Oxford University Press, 1932).

Hess, R.S., 'Smitten Ant Bites Back: Rhetorical Forms in the Amarna Correspondence from Shechem', in de Moor and Watson (eds.), *Verse in Ancient Near Eastern Prose*, pp. 95-111.

Holladay, John S., Jr, 'Assyrian Statecraft and the Prophets of Israel', *HTR* 63 (1970), pp. 29-51.

Hollis, F.J., 'The Sun-Cult and the Temple at Jerusalem', in Hooke (ed.), *Myth and Ritual*, pp. 87-110.

Hooke, S.H. (ed.), *The Labyrinth: Further Studies in the Relation between Myth and Ritual in the Ancient World* (London: SPCK, 1935).

—*Myth and Ritual: Essays on the Myth and Ritual of the Hebrews in Relation to the Culture Pattern of the Ancient East* (London: Oxford University Press, 1933).

—*Myth, Ritual and Kingship: Essays on the Theory and Practice of Kingship in the Ancient Near East and in Israel* (London: Oxford University Press, 1958).

Hughes, G.R., 'A Demotic Letter to Thoth', *JNES* 17 (1958), pp. 1-12.

Jacobsen, Thorkild, 'Mesopotamia', in Frankfort, Frankfort, Wilson and Jacobsen, *Before Philosophy*, pp. 137-234.

Jamieson-Drake, D.W., *Scribes and Schools in Monarchic Judah* (The Social World of Biblical Antiquity, 9; JSOTSup, 109; Sheffield: Almond Press, 1991).

Jirku, A., *Altorientalische Kommentar zum Alten Testament* (Leipzig: A. Deichert, 1923).

—'Kanaanische Psalmenfragmente in der vorisraelitischen Zeit Palästinas und Syriens', *JBL* 52 (1933), pp. 108-20; reprinted in *idem, Von Jerusalem nach Ugarit*, pp. 331-44.

—*Von Jerusalem nach Ugarit* (Graz: Akademische Druck- und Verlagsanstalt, 1966).

Johnson, Aubrey R., 'The Psalms', in Rowley (ed.), *The Old Testament and Modern Study*, pp. 162-209.

—'The Role of the King in the Jerusalem Cultus', in Hooke (ed.), *The Labyrinth*, pp. 71-111.

Kitchen, Kenneth A., *Poetry of Ancient Egypt* (Jonsered: Paul Aström, 1999).

—*Suppiluliuma and the Amarna Pharaohs* (Liverpool Monographs in Archaeological and Oriental Studies; Liverpool: Liverpool University Press, 1962).

Knudtzon, J.A., *Assyrische Gebete an den Sonnengott* (Leipzig: E. Pfeiffer, 1893).

—*Die El-Amarna Tafeln* (Vorderasiatische Bibliothek, 2; 2 vols.; Leipzig: J.C. Hinrichs, 1907–15).

Kramer, S.N., 'Lamentation over the Destruction of Sumer and Ur', in *ANET*, pp. 611-19.

—*Lamentation over the Destruction of Ur* (Assyriological Studies, 12; Chicago: Chicago University Press, 1940).

Kraus, H.-J. *Psalms 1–59* (trans. Hilton C. Oswald; Minneapolis: Augsburg Press, 1988).

Krecher, J., *Sumerische Kultlyrik* (Wiesbaden: Otto Harrassowitz, 1966).

Kunstmann, Walter G., *Die babylonische Gebetsbeschwörung* (Leipziger Semitische Studien, NF 2; Leipzig: J.C. Hinrichs, 1932).

Kutscher, R., *Oh Angry Sea: The History of a Sumerian Congregational Lament* (Yale Near Eastern Researches, 6; New Haven: Yale University Press, 1975).

Labat, R., 'Le rayonnement de la langue et de l'écriture akkadiennes du deuxième millénaire avant notre ère', *Syria* 39 (1962), pp. 1-27.

Laessøe, J., *People of Ancient Assyria* (London: Routledge & Kegan Paul, 1963).

Lambert, W.G., *Babylonian Wisdom Literature* (Oxford: Clarendon Press, 1960).

Landsberger, B., *Brief des Bischofs von Esagila an König Asarhaddon* (Amsterdam: Noord-Hollandsche Uitgevers-Maatschappij, 1965).

—Review of Stummer, *Sumerische-akkadische Parallelen*, *OLZ* (1925), cols. 479-83.

Lanfranchi, G.B., and S. Parpola, *The Correspondence of Sargon II. II. Letters from the Northern and Northeastern Provinces* (SAA, 5; Helsinki: Helsinki University Press, 1990).

Langdon, S., *Babylonian Liturgies* (Paris: Librairie Paul Geuthner, 1913).

—*Sumerian and Babylonian Psalms* (Paris: Librairie Paul Geuthner, 1909).

—*Tammuz and Ishtar* (Oxford: Clarendon Press, 1914).

Lichtheim, M., *Ancient Egyptian Literature* (3 vols.; Berkeley: University of California Press, 1973).

Luckenbill, D.D., 'Hittite Treaties and Letters', *AJSL* 37 (1920–21), pp. 161-211.

Luukko, M., and G. Van Buylaere, *The Political Correspondence of Esarhaddon* (SAA, 16; Helsinki: Helsinki University Press, 2002).

McCann, J.C. (ed.), *The Shape and Shaping of the Psalter* (JSOTSup, 159; Sheffield: Sheffield Academic Press, 1993).

McCarthy, D.J., *Treaty and Covenant: A Study in Form in the Ancient Oriental Documents and in the Old Testament* (AnBib, 21A; Rome: Pontifical Biblical Institute Press, 1963).

McDaniel, T.F., 'The Alleged Sumerian Influence upon Lamentations', *VT* 18 (1968), pp. 198-209.

Mendelsohn, I., 'Samuel's Denunciation of Kingship in the Light of the Akkadian Documents from Ugarit', *BASOR* 143 (1956), pp. 17-22.

Mendenhall, George E., 'Covenant Forms in Israelite Tradition', *BA* 17 (1954), pp. 50-76; reprinted in Campbell and Freedman (eds.), *The Biblical Archaeologist Reader 3*, pp. 25-53.

—'Mari', in Freedman and Campbell (eds.), *Biblical Archaeology Reader 2*, pp. 3-20.

Mercer, S.A.B., *The Tell el-Amarna Tablets* (2 vols.; Toronto: Macmillan, 1939).

Millard, A.R., 'For He is Good', *TynBul* 17 (1966), pp. 115-17.

Miller, Patrick D., *The Divine Warrior in Early Israel* (Harvard Semitic Monographs, 5; Cambridge, MA: Harvard University Press, 1973).

Moor, J.C. de, and W.G.E. Watson, *Verse in Ancient Near Eastern Prose* (AOAT, 42; Kevelaer: Butzon & Bercker; Neukirchen–Vluyn: Neukirchener Verlag, 1993).

Moore, G.F., *Judaism in the First Centuries of the Christian Era: The Age of Tannaim* (3 vols.; Cambridge, MA: Harvard University Press, 1927–30).

Moran, W.L., *The Amarna Letters* (Baltimore: The Johns Hopkins University Press, 1992).

Morenz, S., *Egyptian Religion* (trans. Ann E. Keep; London: Methuen, 1960).

Mowinckel, Sigmund, 'Psalm Criticism between 1900 and 1935 (Ugarit and Psalm Exegesis)', *VT* 5 (1955), pp. 12-33.

—*Psalmenstudien*. I. *Awän und die individuelle Klagepsalmen* (Videnskapsselskapets Skrifter II. Hist.-Filos. Klasse, 1921, 4; Oslo: Dybwad, 1921).

—*The Psalms in Israel's Worship* (trans. D.R. Ap-Thomas; 2 vols.; Oxford: Basil Black-well, 1962).

Muilenburg, J., 'The Form and Structure of the Covenantal Formulations', *VT* 9 (1959), pp. 347-65.

Nicolsky, N., *Spuren magischer Formeln in den Psalmen* (BZAW, 46; Giessen: Alfred Töpelmann, 1927).

North, C.R., 'The Religious Aspects of Hebrew Kingship', *ZAW* 50 (1932), pp. 8-38.

Noth, Martin, *The Laws in the Pentateuch and Other Stuides* (Edinburgh: Oliver & Boyd, 1966).

Nötscher, F., *'Das Angesicht Gottes schauen'* (Würzburg: C.J. Becker, 1924; repr., Darmstadt: Wissenschaftliches Buchgesellschaft, 1969).

Nougayrol, J. *et al.*, *Ugaritica*, V (Mission de Ras Shamra, 16; Paris: Imprimerie Nationale, 1968).

Oesterley, W.O.E., *The Psalms* (London: SPCK, 1939).

Olmstead, A.T., *History of Assyria* (New York: Charles Scribner's Sons, 1923).

Oppenheim, A.L., *Ancient Mesopotamia: Portrait of a Dead Civilization* (Chicago: University of Chicago Press, 1964).

—*Letters from Mesopotamia* (Chicago: University of Chicago Press, 1967).

Pardee, D., *Handbook of Ancient Hebrew Letters* (SBL Sources for Biblical Study, 15; Chico, CA: Scholars Press, 1982).

Parpola, Simo, *Assyrian Prophecies* (SAA, 9; Helsinki: Helsinki University Press, 1997).

—*The Correspondence of Sargon II*. I. *Letters from Assyria and the West* (State Archives of Assyria, 1; Helsinki: Helsinki University Press, 1987).

—*Letters from Assyrian and Babylonian Scholars* (SAA, 10; Helsinki: Helsinki University Press, 1993).

Parrot, A., 'Mari', in *AOTS*, pp. 136-44.

Parrot, A., and G. Dossin, *Archives royales de Mari* (28 vols.; I–IX, Paris: Imprimerie Nationale, 1950–60; X–XXI, Paris: P. Guthner, 1963–83; XXII–XXVIII, Paris: Éditions Recherche sur les Civilisations, 1948–98).

Patton, J.H., *Canaanite Parallels in the Book of Psalms* (Baltimore: The Johns Hopkins University Press, 1944).

Pedersen, J., *Der Eid bei den Semiten* (Studien zur Geschichte und Kultur des Islamischen Orients; Strasbourg: Trübner, 1914).

—*Israel: Its Life and Culture* (London: Oxford University Press; Copenhagen: Branner & Korch, I-II, 1926; III-IV, 1940).

Porter, J.R., 'The Interpretation of 2 Samuel vi and Psalm cxxxii', *JTS* NS 5 (1954), pp. 161-75.

Rainey, A.F., *El Amarna Tablets 359–379* (AOAT, 8; Neukirchen–Vluyn: Neukirchener Verlag, 1978).

Reindl, J., *Das Angesicht Gottes im Spriachgebraush des Alten Testaments* (Erfurter Theologische Studien, 25; Leipzig: St Benno, 1970).

Reventlow, H., 'Kultische Recht im Alten Testament', *ZThK* 60 (1963), pp. 267-304.

Reynolds, F.S., *The Babylonian Correspondence of Esarhaddon and Letters to Assurbanipal and Sin-šarru-iškun from Northern and Central Babylonia* (SAA, 18; Helsinki: Helsinki University Press, 2003).

Ridderbos, N.H., *Die Psalmen: Stilistische Verfahren und Aufbau mit besonderer Berücksichtigung von Ps 1–41* (BZAW, 117; Berlin: W. de Gruyter, 1972).

Ringgren, H., *The Faith of the Psalmists* (London: SCM Press, 1963).

Röllig, W. (ed.), Lišan mithurti. *FS Wolfram Freiherr von Soden zum 19.6.1968 gewidmet van Schülern und Mitarbeiten* (AOAT, 1; Kevelaer: Butzon & Bercker, 1969).

Rowley, H.H. (ed.), *The Old Testament and Modern Study* (Oxford: Clarendon Press, 1951).

Saggs, H.W.F., *The Greatness that was Babylon* (London: Sidgwick & Jackson, 2nd edn, 1988 [1962]).

—*The Might that was Assyria* (London: Sidgwick & Jackson, 1984).

—*The Nimrud Letters 1952* (Cuneiform Texts from Nimrud, 5; British School of Archaeology in Iraq, 2001).

Schaeffer, C.F.A. (ed.), *Le palais royal d'Ugarit*, III and IV (Mission de Ras Shamra, 6 and 9; Paris: Imprimerie Nationale, 1955).

Schmidt, Hans, *Das Gebet der Angeklagten im Alten Testament* (BZAW, 49; Giessen: Alfred Töpelmann, 1928).

—'Das Gebet der Angeklagten im Alten Testament', in Simpson (ed.), *Old Testament Essays*, pp. 143-55.

—*Die Psalmen* (HAT, 15; Tübingen: J.C.B. Mohr [Paul Siebeck], 1934).

Seybold, Klaus, *Introduction to the Psalms* (Edinburgh: T. & T. Clark, 1990).

Simpson, D.C. (ed.), *Old Testament Essays: Papers Read before the Society for Old Testament Study at its Eighteenth Meeting at Keble College Oxford September 27th to 30th, 1927* (London: Charles Griffin, 1927).

—*The Psalmists* (London: Oxford University Press, 1926).

Simpson, W.K., *The Literature of Ancient Egypt* (New Haven: Yale University Press, 1973).

Smend, R., *Die Bundesformel* (Theologische Studien, 68; Zürich: EVZ Verlag, 1963).

Smith, Sidney, 'The Practice of Kingship in Early Semitic Kingdoms', in Hooke (ed.), *Myth, Ritual and Kingship*, pp. 22-73.

Sommer, F. (ed.), *Hethitische Texte in Umschrift* (Mitteilungen der Vorderasiatischen Gesellschaft, 29.3; 31.1; 32.1; 34.1-2; 38; Leipzig: J.C. Hinrichs, 1925–33).

Stamm, J.J., and M.E. Andrew, *The Ten Commandments in Recent Research* (Studies in Biblical Theology, Second Series, 2; London: SCM Press, 1967).

Starr, Ivan, *Queries to the Sungod: Divination and Politics in Sargonid Assyria* (SAA, 4; Helsinki: Helsinki University Press, 1990).

Streck, M., *Assurbanipal und die letzten assyrischen Königs bis zum Untergange Nineveh's* (VAB, 7; Leipzig: J.C. Hinrichs, 1916).

Stummer, F., *Sumerische-akkadische Parallelen zum Aufbau alttestamentichen Psalmen* (Studien zur Geschichte und Kultur des Altertums, 11; Paderborn: Schöningh, 1922).

Thomas, D. Winton (ed.), *Documents from Old Testament Times* (London: Nisbet, 1958).

Thomas, D. Winton, and W.D. McHardy (eds.), *Hebrew and Semitic Studies Presented to Godfrey Rolles Driver* (Oxford: Oxford University Press, 1963).

Thompson, J.A., *The Ancient Near Eastern Treaties and the Old Testament* (London: Tyndale Press, 1964).

Tomes, Roger, 'The Psalms', in Bigger (ed.), *Creating the Old Testament*, pp. 251-67.

Vaux, R. de, *Ancient Israel: Its Life and Institutions* (trans. J. McHugh; London: Darton, Longman & Todd, 1961).

Veenhof, K.R., '"Seeing the Face of God": The Use of Akkadian Parallels', *Akkadica* 94–95 (1995), pp. 33-37.

Waterman, L., *Royal Correspondence of the Assyrian Empire* (University of Michigan Studies, Humanistic Series, 17-20; Ann Arbor: University of Michigan Press, 1930–36).

Weber, O., 'Anmerkungen von O. Weber', in Knudtzon, *Die El-Amarna Tafeln*, II, pp. 1009-57.

Weidner, E.F., *Politische Documente aus Kleinasien: Die Staatsverträge in akkadischer Sprache aus dem Archiv aus Boghazköi* (Boghazköi-Studien, 8-9; Leipzig: J.C. Hinrichs, 1923).

Weiser, A., 'Zur Frage nach den Beziehungen der Psalmen zum Kult: Die Darstellung der Theophanie in den Psalmen und im Festkult', in Baumgartner, Eissfeldt, Elliger and Rost (eds.), *Festschrift für Alfred Bertholet*, pp. 513-31; reprinted in *idem, Glaube und Geschichte im Alten Testament* (Göttingen: Vandenhoeck & Ruprecht, 1961), pp. 303-21.

—*The Psalms* (trans. H. Hartwell; OTL; London: SCM Press, 1962).

Wendel, A., *Das freie Laiengebet in vorexilischen Israel* (Leipzig: E. Pfeiffer, 1931).

Westermann, Claus, 'Struktur und Geschichte der Klage im Alten Testament', *ZAW* 66 (1954), pp. 44-80; reprinted in *idem, Forschung am Alten Testament*, pp. 266-305; ET *Praise and Lament in the Psalms*, pp. 165-258.

—*Forschung am Alten Testament. Gesammelte Studien I* (TBü, 24; Munich: Chr. Kaiser Verlag, 1964).

—*Das Loben Gottes in den Psalmen* (Göttingen: Vandenhoeck & Ruprecht, 2nd edn, 1961); ET *The Praise of God in the Psalms*; reprinted in *Praise and Lament in the Psalms*, pp. 15-162.

—*The Praise of God in the Psalms* (trans. K.R. Crim; London: Epworth Press, 1966).

—*Praise and Lament in the Psalms* (trans. K.R. Crim and R.N. Soulen; Edinburgh: T. & T. Clark, 1981).

Widengren, Geo, *The Akkadian and Hebrew Psalms of Lamentation as Religious Documents: A Comparative Study* (Stockholm: Bokförlags Aktiebolaget Thule, 1937).

Williams, R.J., 'The Hymn to Aten', in *DOTT*, pp. 142-50.

Wilson, G.H., *The Editing of the Hebrew Psalter* (SBLDS, 76; Chico, CA: Scholars Press, 1985).

Wiseman, D.J., 'Alalakh', in Thomas (ed.), *Archaeology and Old Testament Study*, pp. 119-35.

—*The Alalakh Tablets* (Occasional Publications of the British Institute of Archaeology in Ankara, 2; London: British Institute of Archaeology at Ankara 1953).

—*The Vassal Treaties of Esarhaddon* (London: British School of Archaeology in Iraq, 1958 [= *Iraq* 20]).

Woude, A.S. van der, 'פָּנִים, *panîm*, Angesicht', in *THAT*, cols. 432-60.

Wright, G. Ernest, *Biblical Archaeology* (London: Gerald Duckworth, 1956).

—*Shechem: Biography of a Biblical City* (London: Gerald Duckworth, 1965).

—'The Terminology of Old Testament Religion and its Significance', *JNES* 1 (1942), pp. 404-14.

INDEXES

INDEX OF REFERENCES

SAHG (cont.)		B 44	40, 42,	B 58	45
B 17	33, 45,		45, 53, 54	B 61	33, 40,
	46, 61	B 45	42, 45, 54		45, 61, 84
B 18	45	B 46	42, 45,	B 64	84
B 19	40		53, 54		
B 24-38	13	B 47	42, 45, 54	*Tale of Sinuhe*	
B 39	89	B 50	42, 46, 54	—	73
B 40	45	B 51	42, 54,		
B 40-81	13		71, 84	*Turin*	
B 41	42, 54, 64	B 52	91	102	38
B 43	40, 41,	B 53-58	78		
	45, 46, 53	B 56	45		

INDEX OF MODERN AUTHORS

INDEX OF SUBJECTS

Index of Names

Printed in the United Kingdom
by Lightning Source UK Ltd.
111398UKS00001B/268-303

9 781905 048717